THE ART OF MARRIAGE

JEWISH LEARNING INSTITUTE

ב"ד

The **Rohr Jewish Learning Institute**
gratefully acknowledges
the pioneering support of

George and Pamela Rohr

SINCE ITS INCEPTION,
the **Rohr JLI** has been
a beneficiary of the vision, generosity,
care, and concern
of the **Rohr family**

In the merit of
the tens of thousands of hours of Torah study
by **JLI** students worldwide,
may they be blessed with health,
Yiddishe nachas from all their loved ones,
and extraordinary success
in all their endeavors ﻉﻝ

The Art of Marriage
course is dedicated
in honor of

Rebecca Rohr

רבקה מלכה

&

Harry Ritter

יצחק צבי

ON THE OCCASION OF THEIR FORTHCOMING WEDDING

*May Hashem shower His abundant blessings upon them,
and may they share a long life of peace, health, and happiness together.
May they be a source of nachas to their parents, grandparents,
and all of Klal Yisrael.*

Dedicated by the staff, faculty, and thousands of students worldwide of the
Rohr Jewish Learning Institute

Tag is an organization dedicated to promoting the broadest possible contribution of Jews and Judaism to the improvement of the world. We believe that the social values of Judaism and the rich experience of Jewish life offer a source of wisdom that can help address social challenges facing people today.

Tag Institute contributes to innovative, evidence-based solutions to pressing social issues by conducting research in the social sciences that is informed by ideas, values, and practices found in traditional Jewish sources.

Recent research and projects have addressed, amongst others, the following areas:

- **Bullying and social exclusion**
- **Aging enrichment**
- **Values-based parenting**
- **Moral education for adolescents**
- **Singles' relationship issues**
- **Spirituality and anxiety disorders**

The development of this course
was made possible by a grant from

Tag Institute for Jewish Social Values

A think tank and research center that seeks to harness
Jewish heritage, knowledge, and ideas to benefit
individuals and the wider society.

Endorsements for *The Art of Marriage*

"**B**eautiful, inspiring, but most of all *practical*—these words describe this vital course from the Rohr Jewish Learning Institute. Whether your marriage is magical or miserable, this course is designed for you."

Pat Love, EdD
Author/co-author of five books, including
How to Improve Your Marriage Without Talking About It

"**T**his important course from the Rohr Jewish Learning Institute helps teach all of us 'the art and science of marriage.' Research clearly shows the benefits of marriage for individuals and for society. Married people have better health—both mental and physical—than people who are not married. Their children do better on almost any measure we consider. Countries with more families headed by a married couple have less crime and higher productivity. So how do we achieve a stable marriage? What role does physical intimacy play? What can we do to keep our marriages healthy and happy? This course will address these important issues from a Jewish perspective. It looks terrific!"

Linda J. Waite, PhD
Lucy Flower Professor, Department of Sociology & Senior Fellow, NORC, University of Chicago
Author of *The Case for Marriage* and *The Ties that Bind*

"**T**he Rohr Jewish Learning Institute, which consistently offers relevant and well-presented courses on life's central issues, has created a program that will enhance individuals' most fundamental relationships. The topics covered by this series are crucial, and understanding time-tested means of approaching them is sure to improve even the most solid and loving marriages."

Dr. Diane Medved, PhD
Clinical psychologist
Author of *The Case Against Divorce*

"**O**nce again, the Rohr Jewish Learning Institute has come up with a course that is not only informative but practical for all. *The Art of Marriage* has the ability to illuminate the way to the 'lighthouse' of marital life. It will empower couples to maneuver safely in the tumultuous storms that sometimes accompany real life. Hats off to the Rohr Jewish Learning Institute for this initiative!"

Rus Devorah (Darcy) Wallen, LCSW, ACSW
Clinical consultant, psychotherapist, motivational entertainer

"**D**uring these times, when the institute of marriage is being questioned by our society, *The Art of Marriage* will shed light on the reasons for getting married and teach the skills needed to turn a good relationship into a great one. *The Art of Marriage* represents a breakthrough in presenting the case for marriage from Jewish and scientific sources and for achieving a healthy and long-lasting marriage."

Rabbi Daniel Schonbuch, MA
Marriage and family therapist

"With marriages crumbling all around us, this course will strengthen a couple's ability to respect and accept each other and give them tools to fight the insidious effects of drugs, infidelity, the Internet, and other addictions."

Dr. Miriam Adahan, PhD
Psychologist, therapist, founder of EMETT
Author of *Appreciate People*

"*The Art of Marriage* offers timeless spiritual and practical Jewish wisdom about all stages and phases of marriage. Taking this class may be the best investment you will ever make for a lifelong fulfilling relationship with your spouse."

Marcia Naomi Berger, MSW, LCSW
Author of *Marriage Meeting Starter Kit*

Table of Contents

1

Lesson **1**
The Case for Marriage
Antiquated Relic vs. Existential Need

25

Lesson **2**
Bedroom Secrets
A Jewish View on Intimacy

57

Lesson **3**
Will My Spouse Ever Change?
What You Can Do About Character Flaws

87

Lesson **4**
Becoming a Better Half
What is a *Mensch*?

115

Lesson **5**
Sacred Space: No Trespassing!
Defining Marriage's Boundaries

147

Lesson **6**
Make Up or Break Up
Negotiating the Most Significant Challenge
of Our Generation

Lesson 1
The Case for Marriage
Antiquated Relic vs. Existential Need
Introduction

Though marriage has been part and parcel of the human condition since the dawn of mankind, in recent times, many an enlightened voice has argued that the marital institution is a relic of the age of patriarchy. Indeed, society has changed and many of the traditional reasons for getting married have gone by the wayside, prompting many to predict the demise of marriage. Is there still reason to marry?

The State of the Union
Why Marry?

Learning Interaction 1

"Marriage is a wonderful institution, but who wants to live in an institution?"

—Groucho Marx

Indicate your level of agreement with this statement, with 1 meaning you totally disagree and 10 meaning you totally agree.

1   2   3   4   5   6   7   8   9   10

Learning Interaction 2

In your estimation, what are the three primary reasons that people seek marriage? Choose from the following list or add your own reason(s).

❏ Admiration	❏ Financial security	❏ Satisfaction
❏ Attachment	❏ Friendship	❏ Serenity
❏ Being part of a nuclear family	❏ Having children	❏ Sexual intimacy
❏ Company	❏ Love	❏ Shared purpose
❏ Compatibility	❏ Meeting social expectations	❏ Tax benefits
❏ Emotional security	❏ Passion	❏ Trust
❏ _____	❏ _____	❏ _____

Question for Discussion

Carefully consider your three choices. Without being married, is it possible to gain the same or similar benefits in the course of a loving, close, monogamous relationship with a member of the opposite gender?

Marriage by the Numbers

Learning Interaction 3

True or False:

1. The probability that an American will marry by the age of forty is higher than 80 percent. *True / False*

2. College graduates are more likely to marry than those with no higher education. *True / False*

3. More than one-third of Americans under the age of thirty assert that they don't feel the need to marry. *True / False*

4. More than two-thirds of romantic partners who live together claim to be happy and have no intention of marrying. *True / False*

Text 1

Belinda Luscombe. Australian-born journalist, senior editor for *Time* magazine since April 1999, named arts editor in January 2003. In 2010, she was awarded The Council on Contemporary Families Media Award for Print Coverage of Family Issues.

Neither men nor women need to be married to have sex or companionship or professional success or respect or even children—yet marriage remains revered and desired.

Belinda Luscombe, "Who Needs Marriage? A Changing Institution," *Time*, Nov. 18, 2010

Kidushin and *Nisu'in*

Text 2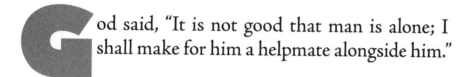

וַיֹּאמֶר ה׳ אֱלֹקִים, "לֹא טוֹב הֱיוֹת הָאָדָם לְבַדּוֹ, אֶעֱשֶׂה לּוֹ עֵזֶר כְּנֶגְדּוֹ".
בראשית ב,יח

God said, "It is not good that man is alone; I shall make for him a helpmate alongside him."

Genesis 2:18

Text 3

We . . . live best in the shelter offered by another's love. An attachment bond is persistent. Once made, it is specific to another "irreplaceable" person. Once we are bonded, we seek out closeness with our loved one and we are deeply distressed at emotional or physical separation. We seek comfort and a sense of security with this person. . . . We are emotionally invested in these relationships and they penetrate key aspects of our lives. These bonds have incredible survival value. We are healthier, happier, psychologically stronger, and we live longer when we are close and connected. . . .

This is why, even though we might get distracted into a one night sexual adventure, we still fight to connect and to hold onto our love relationships. Our most natural

Dr. Sue Johnson is the director of the International Center for Excellence in Emotionally Focused Therapy and distinguished research professor at Alliant University in San Diego, California, as well as professor of clinical psychology at the University of Ottawa, Canada. Johnson is one of the developers of Emotionally Focused Therapy (EFT). She has written many books and articles, including the best seller *Hold Me Tight*.

and longed for state is a strong, nurturing monogamous pair bond.

Sue Johnson, "Is Monogamy Just a Myth or Is It Possible?" www.holdmetight.com

Text 4a

כיון שנתנה תורה נצטוו ישראל שאם ירצה האיש לישא אשה יקנה אותה תחלה בפני עדים ואחר כך תהיה לו לאשה.

משנה תורה, הלכות אישות א,א

Rabbi Moshe ben Maimon (1135–1204). Better known as Maimonides or by the acronym Rambam; born in Cordoba, Spain. After the conquest of Cordoba by the Almohads, he fled Spain and eventually settled in Cairo, Egypt. There, he became the leader of the Jewish community and served as court physician to the vizier of Egypt. His rulings on Jewish law are considered integral to the formation of halachic consensus. He is most noted for authoring the *Mishneh Torah,* an encyclopedic arrangement of Jewish law, and for his philosophical work, *Guide for the Perplexed.*

When the Torah was given, God instructed the Jews that if a man wishes to marry a woman, he must first acquire her [hand in marriage] in the presence of witnesses, and afterwards she can be his wife.

Maimonides, *Mishneh Torah,* Laws of Marriage 1:1

Text 4b 📖

הארוסה אסורה לבעלה . . . עד שיביא אותה לתוך ביתו ויתיחד עמה ויפרישנה לו . . .
והוא הנקרא נישואין.

שם י,א

A betrothed couple may not be sexually intimate . . . until the groom secludes himself
with the bride in his home and designates
her [as his wife]. . . . This is called *nisu'in*.

Ibid., 10:1

Questions **for Discussion**

**1. Why would the Torah mandate a period when the couple is mar-
ried—but may not enjoy a marital relationship?**

**2. What *is* marriage if not a relationship between a man and wom-
an? In the absence of the relationship and what it has to offer, by
what virtue is it marriage?**

1+1=1
In the Footsteps of Adam and Eve

Question for Discussion

Which relationship is deeper, the relationship between spouses or the parent-child relationship? What is your reasoning?

Text 5 📖

וַיַּפֵּל ה׳ אֱלֹקִים תַּרְדֵּמָה עַל הָאָדָם וַיִּישָׁן, וַיִּקַּח אַחַת מִצַּלְעֹתָיו וַיִּסְגֹּר בָּשָׂר תַּחְתֶּנָה. וַיִּבֶן ה׳ אֱלֹקִים אֶת הַצֵּלָע אֲשֶׁר לָקַח מִן הָאָדָם לְאִשָּׁה, וַיְבִאֶהָ אֶל הָאָדָם. וַיֹּאמֶר הָאָדָם, "זֹאת הַפַּעַם עֶצֶם מֵעֲצָמַי וּבָשָׂר מִבְּשָׂרִי".

בראשית ב,כא–כג

God caused a deep slumber to fall upon the man, and he slept. God removed one of his sides, and sealed flesh in its place. God built the side that He had taken from the man [and fashioned it] into a woman, and He brought her to the man.

The man said, "At last, a bone from my bone and flesh from my flesh."

Genesis 2:21–23

Text 6a

בההיא שעתא דאפיק קודשא בריך הוא נשמתין לעלמא, כל אינון רוחין ונשמתין
כלהו כלילן דכר ונוקבא דמתחברן כחדא . . . ובשעתא דנחתין . . . מתפרשין . . .
וכד מטא עידן דזווגא דלהון, קודשא בריך הוא דידע אינון רוחין ונשמתין מחבר לון
כדבקדמיתא . . . וכד אתחברן, אתעבידו חד גופא חד נשמתא.

זוהר א, צא,ב

When God sends forth souls into the world, each includes a male and a female joined together. . . . When they descend to the world . . . they are separated from each other. . . .

When their time to be married arrives, God, Who knows these souls, joins them as they were before [they descended to this world]. . . . When they are joined together, they become one body and one soul.

Zohar 1:91b

Zohar. The most seminal work of Kabbalah, Jewish mysticism. It is a mystical commentary on the Torah, written in Aramaic and Hebrew. According to Arizal, the Zohar consists of the teachings of Rabbi Shimon bar Yocha'i who lived in the Land of Israel during the 2nd century. The Zohar has become one of the indispensable texts of traditional Judaism, alongside and nearly equal in stature to the Mishnah and Talmud.

Text 6b

עַל כֵּן יַעֲזָב אִישׁ אֶת אָבִיו וְאֶת אִמּוֹ, וְדָבַק בְּאִשְׁתּוֹ וְהָיוּ לְבָשָׂר אֶחָד.

בראשית ב,כד

Therefore, man shall leave his father and mother and cleave to his wife, and they shall become one flesh.

Genesis 2:24

Text 6c

אשתו גופו הואי.

תלמוד בבלי, כתובות סה,ב

One's wife is considered as one's own body.

Talmud, Ketubot 65b

Babylonian Talmud. A literary work of monumental proportions that draws upon the totality of the legal, spiritual, intellectual, ethical, and historical traditions of Judaism, the Babylonian Talmud was set up as a commentary to the Mishnah and was written primarily in Aramaic. The Talmud contains the teachings of the Jewish sages, mostly from the period after the destruction of the Second Temple through the fifth century C.E. The Babylonian Talmud has served as the primary vehicle for the education of countless Jews over the centuries; it is the entry point for all subsequent legal, ethical, and theological Jewish scholarship.

Text 7

"עצם מעצמי ובשר מבשרי וגו' על כן יעזוב איש את אביו ואת אמו וגו'".
רוצה בו, על כן נבראת עצם מעצמיו להיות הדבקות בהם אמת וחזק יותר מדבקות
הבן לאב ולאם שהוא מגופם, כי זה יותר דבק שנלקח חלק ממש מאבריו.
שאלות ותשובות הרשב"א, ח"א סי' ס

"A bone from my bone and flesh from my flesh, etc. Therefore a man leaves his father and mother and cleaves to his wife, etc."

Eve was created from Adam's bone, so that the attachment [between husband and wife] would be truer and more powerful than the attachment between children and their parents, though they come from their parents' bodies. Yet the attachment [between husband and wife] is deeper, for Eve was taken literally from Adam's limbs.

Rabbi Shlomo ben Aderet, *Responsa* 1:60

Rabbi Shlomo ben Aderet (1235–1310). A medieval Spanish rabbi, Talmudist, and authority on Jewish law, widely known by the acronym "Rashba." More than 3,000 of his responsa are extant. In one famous responsum, he responds to the defamatory charges against the Jews, voiced by the Dominican friar Ramón Martí, author of *Pugio Fidei*. Among his numerous students were Ritva, Rabbeinu Bechaye, and Re'ah.

Betrothed—Forever

Text 8a 📜

ברוך אתה ה׳ . . . אשר קדשנו במצותיו וצונו על העריות, ואסר לנו את הארוסות
והתיר לנו את הנשואות לנו על ידי חפה וקדושין.

ברכת אירוסין

Blessed are You, God . . . Who sanctified us with His commandments and instructed us [to refrain from engaging in] illicit relationships; He has forbidden unto us betrotheds and permitted unto us those whom we marry through *chupah* and [the preceding] *kidushin*.

Text of the Betrothal Blessing

Text 8b 📜

היכן מצינו ברכה על השלילה, על מה שאסר לנו?

אבל באמת בשלילה זו יש החיוב הכי גדול. ״ואסר לנו את הארוסות״, שזאת אומרת
כי היא ארוסה אף על פי שהיא אסורה, ועל כרחך שיש זיקה נפשית ורוחנית, זיקה
אצילית ופנימית בין שני אנשים מבלי שום נגיעה ופניה חיצונית, שעל זה יש באמת לברך.

הגיונות אל עמי חלק ב׳, ע׳ מא

Where do we find the recitation of a blessing on a negative, on something that God forbade?

In truth, however, this "negative" isn't negative at all. The words, "He has forbidden unto us betrotheds" reveals a

Rabbi Moshe Avigdor Amiel (1883–1946). Rabbi, religious thinker, and author, student of Rabbi Chaim Soloveichik and Rabbi Chaim Ozer Grodzinski. A chief ideologue of religious Zionism, Amiel was elected chief rabbi of Tel Aviv in 1936. Amiel's first halachic publication was *Darchei Moshe,* followed by his three-volume *Hamidot Lecheker Hahalachah.* A renowned preacher, he published the homiletic works *Derashot El Ami* and *Hegyonot El Ami.*

paradox: the woman is betrothed, yet she is forbidden to her husband. It must be then that the couple shares a profound soulful and spiritual bond that transcends any physical expression and is not contingent on external benefit. This, indeed, is reason to recite a blessing!

Rabbi Moshe Avigdor Amiel, *Hegyonot El Ami* 2:41

Text 9a

וְאֵרַשְׂתִּיךְ לִי לְעוֹלָם.

וְאֵרַשְׂתִּיךְ לִי בְּצֶדֶק וּבְמִשְׁפָּט וּבְחֶסֶד וּבְרַחֲמִים.

וְאֵרַשְׂתִּיךְ לִי בֶּאֱמוּנָה.

הושע ב,כא–כב

I will betroth you to Me forever.

I will betroth you to Me with righteousness, with justice, with loving-kindness, and with mercy.

I will betroth you to Me with faith.

Hosea 2:21–22

Text 9b

אַף עַל פִּי שֶׁהַנִּשּׂוּאִים הֵם יוֹתֵר נֶעֱרָכִים בִּדְבֵקוּת מֵהָאֵירוּסִין, מִכָּל מָקוֹם יֵשׁ מַעֲלָה בָּאֵירוּסִין, שֶׁהֵם מַבִּיעִים אֶת הַיְסוֹד הַחֻקִּי הָאֲצִילִי שֶׁבַּדְּבֵקוּת הָאֱלֹקִית, שֶׁמִּתּוֹךְ מַעֲלָתוֹ אֵין בּוֹ הַתְפָּסָה לְחִקּוּי חָמְרִי כְּלָל.

וְדַוְקָא הַחֹק הָעֶלְיוֹן הַזֶּה הוּא שֶׁאֵינֶנּוּ מְקַבֵּל שׁוּם שִׁנּוּי, כִּי אֵינֶנּוּ תָּלוּי בְּשׁוּם יַחַשׂ הֶעָלוּל לְהִשְׁתַּנּוּת, כִּי אִם הוּא עוֹמֵד בְּעֶצֶם צִבְיוֹן הַחֹק, שֶׁאִי אֶפְשָׁר כְּלָל לְצַיֵּיר אֹפֶן אַחֵר.

וְזֹאת הַדְּבֵקוּת הַשִּׂכְלִית הַבָּאָה מִצַּד הַהַכָּרָה, בְּהִתְגַּלּוֹתָהּ פַּעַם אַחַת בִּבְהִירוּתָהּ, אֵינֶנָּה עֲלוּלָה לְקַבֵּל שׁוּם שִׁנּוּי כְּלָל, וְנִמְצָא שֶׁהִיא קַיֶּמֶת לְעוֹלָם.

וְאֵרַשְׂתִּיךְ לִי לְעוֹלָם.

עוֹלַת רְאִיָּה א, סֵדֶר תְּפִלִּין ע׳ לה

The *nisu'in* relationship is more valued than *kidushin*, yet *kidushin* holds a distinct advantage: It is the spiritual foundation of the divine union, as decreed by God's law. Intangible by virtue of its exaltedness, it defies physical expression.

This Godly law is not susceptible to fluctuation, for it depends not on change-prone human relationship. It stands firm, colored only by the immutability of the law. It cannot even be envisioned otherwise.

This spiritual attachment—born not of experience, but of simple recognition—need be revealed only once, in its resplendent intensity. And never again is it subject to vacillation. It is everlasting.

"And I will betroth you to Me forever."

Rabbi Avraham Yitschak Hakohen Kook, *Olat Re'iyah*, vol. 1, *Seder Tefilin*, p. 35

Rabbi Avraham Yitschak Hakohen Kook (1864–1935). Main ideologue of the Religious Zionist movement and one of the renowned Torah scholars of the 20th century. Born in Griva, Latvia, he emigrated to Israel in 1904. In 1917, he was appointed rabbi of Jerusalem, and in 1921, he became the first Ashkenazic chief rabbi of pre-state Israel. His influence and outreach created greater respect for Torah and Jewish law in the secular Zionist agricultural settlements.

The Journey That Is Marriage
The Antidote to Loneliness

Text **10a**

Thomas Wolfe (1900–1938). American writer best known for his autobiographical novel, *Look Homeward, Angel* (1929). His novella, *I Have a Thing to Tell You,* addressed the antisemitism and fascism he witnessed during a visit to Germany. In response, Wolfe's writings were banned from Germany. He remains an important writer in modern American literature, inasmuch as he was one of the first masters of autobiographical fiction.

The whole conviction of my life now rests upon the belief that loneliness, far from being a rare and curious phenomenon, peculiar to myself and to a few other solitary men, is the central and inevitable fact of human existence. When we examine the moments, acts, and statements of all kinds of people—not only the grief and ecstasy of the greatest poets, but also the huge unhappiness of the average soul . . . we find, I think, that they are all suffering from the same thing. The final cause of their complaint is loneliness.

Thomas Wolfe, "God's Lonely Man," in Whit Burnett (ed.), *The Spirit of Man* [New York: Hawthorn Books, 1958], p. 20

Text 10b

Ships that pass in the night, and speak each other in passing,

Only a signal shown, and a distant voice in the darkness;

So on the ocean of life, we pass and speak one another,

Only a look and a voice, then darkness again and a silence.

Henry Wadsworth Longfellow, "The Theologian's Tale: Elizabeth," IV, in *Tales of a Wayside Inn*, part III (1873)

Henry Wadsworth Longfellow (1807–1882). Most popular American poet of the 19th century, he presided over Harvard's modern-language program for 18 years. His poem, "Paul Revere's Ride," created an American legend.

Text 11

גם אם האדם נמצא בחברתם של אלפי בני אדם, עדיין נקרא "בודד" כל זמן שהוא בלא אשה, משום שגם אלפי "לבדים" אינם מסוגלים להוציא אף אחד מהם מכלל "לבדיותו" . . . אלא אם כן נתחבר לו משהו בתוך עצמיותו, ואז גם כשגופו יחיד במדבר איננו בודד, משום שבתוך אישיותו קבועה העזר כנגדו, האשה.

אוצר מנהגי נישואין, ע׳ לג

So long as a person is not married, even when he finds himself in the company of thousands of others, he is still "alone"; for a gathering of thousands of "alone" individuals does not solve the loneliness of any one of them. [Loneliness is resolved] only when one attaches to another on an essential level. When one accomplishes this, even if he is alone in the desert, he is not alone, for within his being is embedded his helpmate, his wife.

Rabbi Elyakum Dvorkes, *Otsar Minhagei Nisu'in*, p. 33

Rabbi Elyakum Dvorkes. Noted author of more than ten volumes pertaining to halachah, he resides in Bnei Brak, Israel, and teaches at Yeshivah Tiferet Moshe.

Kidushin Moments

Text 12

The mandatory monthly separation fosters feelings of longing and desire—at the very least, a sense of appreciation—which is followed by the excitement of reunion.

Over the course of a lifetime, open-ended sexual availability may well lead to a waning of excitement and even interest. The monthly hiatus teaches couples to treasure the time they have together and gives them something to look forward to when they are apart. Every month they are separated—not always when convenient or easy—but they wait for one another. They count the days until their togetherness, and each time there is a new quality to their reunion. In this regard the Talmud (Nidah 31b) states: "So that she will be as beloved as on the day of her marriage."

Rivkah Slonim, *Total Immersion: A Mikvah Anthology* [Northvale, N.J.: Jason Aronson, 1996], p. 32

Rivkah Slonim. Noted scholar and lecturer, Slonim is the education director at the Chabad Center for Jewish Student Life at Binghamton University, one of the largest campus Chabad centers. Slonim co-authored the JLI course *Fascinating Facts* and is editor of *Total Immersion: A Mikvah Anthology* and *Bread and Fire: Jewish Women Find God in the Everyday.*

קִידּוּשִׁין

Learning Interaction 4

Think of a stressful marriage scenario. For example:

Men: You arrive home, eat dinner, and are working at the computer on a deadline for a big client while your wife watches Oprah on TV. She calls to you to put the toddler to sleep.

Women: Your husband is good at talking the talk and getting the big clients, but bad at holding on to them and handling the details. So he involves you more and more in the business. Then, when your kid is sent home for cutting class and smoking dope, your husband screams at you: "You're not available to them as a mother!"

What would be your normal reaction?

_____

_____

_____

_____

_____

Now, imagine you had a "*kidushin* moment" before that scenario. How would you reframe what transpired in the larger scheme of things?

_____

_____

_____

_____

_____

Torah Therapy

Question for Discussion

Based on what we've learned in this lesson, what can a couple experiencing difficulty in their marriage gain from consulting a spiritual mentor, such as a rabbi?

Key Points

1. While many believe that marriage is becoming obsolete, an overwhelming majority of people personally plan on getting married and do get married.

2. There's a deep-seated human need for a committed, mutually exclusive relationship with another. This relationship has numerous emotional and psychological benefits. This symbiotic relationship is known as *nisu'in*.

3. There exists an even deeper dimension to the marital relationship, one that makes it unique among all relationships: a husband and wife are two halves of one whole.

4. *Kidushin* symbolizes the essential unity of the couple, because during the *kidushin* period, the relationship between husband and wife is not contingent upon any benefits.

5. A person's natural loneliness can only be resolved by connecting to another on this essential *kidushin* level.

6. Marriage is the most critical relationship in life. A person who does not appreciate this will never realize the full potential of marriage.

7. The laws of family purity allow a couple to renew the excitement of marriage and experience the *kidushin-nisu'in* dynamic on a monthly basis. Furthermore, frequent "*kidushin* moments" enable us to properly cope with marital challenges.

Additional Readings

Is Monogamy Just a Myth or Is It Possible?

by **Dr. Sue Johnson**

Is it natural for human beings to live a monogamous existence? When I ask this question, people look at me with surprise and answer derisively. A colleague from Europe tells me, "Oh, no-one is getting married these days. They are just so discouraged. What is the point? Monogamy is unrealistic, impossible." My friend mutters, "It's about time we gave up on that one! It's a myth." So when I am asked this very question by a television host, I take a very deep breath before I answer, "YES. I think we are naturally monogamous." You can hear jaws dropping everywhere. Cynicism wins hands down. And yet we still glory in the ideal of monogamy. We spend fortunes on whiter than white weddings and act much of the time like the 90% of teenagers in a recent study, who affirm that they hope to marry and remain with the same partner till death do them part! Are we deliberately delusional and setting ourselves up for heartbreak and failure?

The easiest rock to sling at the big M word is that the media is awash with news about people having affairs. Brief sexual dalliances do indeed occur in nearly all socially monogamous animals like the grey wolf or great northern loons who nevertheless prefer to mate and bond with one partner at a time. In our species, some surveys have wildly exaggerated the occurrence of affairs. Reliable studies suggest that around 25% of men and 11% of women will end up in bed with someone other than their partner at some point in their lives. The mundane fact that most of us do not have affairs is overshadowed by titillating public stories of intrigue and deception.

A more basic argument against monogamy is the theory that affairs are, in fact, inevitable precisely because sex is the most powerful instinct of all. Men in particular, as this theory goes, are sex addicts at heart. Given any opportunity at all, they are wired by evolution to pass on as many of their genes as possible and so achieve a kind of immortality. Oh please! This is a long way from more mundane motivations whispered in the pick up lines that I can remember. Having worked with and researched distressed couples for 30 years, I am more convinced by the view that most affairs are the result either of unbearable loneliness that happens when we don't know how to make love work, or of preemptive attempts to grab at a loving monogamous bond when the one we are in seems to be dying and taking us with it.

The second apparent nail in the coffin of monogamy is that we do indeed divorce. About a third or more of us (and yes, the rate is going down in North America) don't make it to the "death do us part" bit, especially if you marry young. But so-called serial monogamy is still monogamy, even if, like everything else, it's not absolute and for all time. I think the divorce rates simply mean that most of us just don't know how to get it right—we don't understand how to create a strong loving bond. We try desperately to dance a love-you-forever tango often without ever having even seen the steps! As a couple therapist, I see how intently invested partners are in this struggle on a daily basis. And when we fail, most often we find another partner and keep right on trying!

There are other arguments against monogamy. One is that polygamy dominates in many cultures. Romantic love, however, seems to exist everywhere and given half the chance, rears up and takes over. When people have a choice and do not have to marry out of fear or just to survive, they marry for love. They choose to bond with a special other. But, some naturalists say, only 7% of mammals are socially monogamous. My response is, "Yes and we are one of those 7%." It is accepted by scientists that 90% of birds are monogamous, even though birds, like seagulls, have about a 25% divorce rate. The arguments are probably different in seagull couples though. They might go, "That stick you found does not go with the *feng shui* tone of this nest." Some animals are actually better at monogamy than us! The pygmy marmoset is faithful, dedicated, and shares symptoms of pregnancy with his lady. The Californian mouse is socially and sexually monogamous and this matters; if the babies aren't cuddled constantly by Mr. Mouse they don't make it.

Now we come to the reasons for my belief that monogamy, based on deep bonds of romantic love, is natural for humans. First, monogamy shows up in animals who invest time and work in rearing their kids and dealing with survival challenges. Beavers work as a team to rear young, build dams and gather food. They have to coordinate their movements, synchronize efforts, and read each other's cues. They depend on each other, and this is an important word, depend.

The second and most potent argument for monogamy is that we are wired for it! A huge part of our brain is designed not just for social group interaction but for the intimate synchrony of emotional connection and bonding. The pacing, the give and take, the tuning in, the adapting to the other's emotional cues between parents and infants and between adult lovers, are all about bonding. The main message of the new science of adult bonding is that the instinct to reach, connect and rely on loved ones is primary, more fundamental even than sex. Monogamous mammals like us have special cuddle hormones like oxytocin or OT—the so called molecule of monogamy. It turns off stress hormones, turns on reward centers, and fills us with calm contentment and well-being. OT is released at orgasm and even when simply thinking of our partner! When primed with this hormone, our brains find it easier to tune into another person and read intentions. When scientists increase OT in little monogamous prairie voles, they cuddle more and mate less. When they block OT, they mate but don't cuddle. Our brains are wired for a certain kind of connection with those we depend on. As the Dali Lama suggests, human affection is the one indispensable necessity in life.

We are bonding animals who live best in the shelter offered by another's love. An attachment bond is persistent. Once made, it is specific to another "irreplaceable" person. Once we are bonded, we seek out closeness with our loved one and we are deeply distressed at emotional or physical separation. We seek comfort and a sense of security with this person. We can have more than one bond of course. But for most of us, there is a hierarchy of one or two loved ones, and our sexual partner is usually at the top of the list. We are emotionally invested in these relationships and they penetrate key aspects of our lives. These bonds have incredible survival value. We are healthier, happier, psychologically stronger, and we live longer when we are close and connected. This deep desire to matter to another, to be able to turn to another as a safe haven, gets lost in our culture of mine, me and myself. We forget to mention that being the best you can be inevitably involves being connected to somebody else! We are not meant for so called self-sufficiency and the emotional isolation that comes with it.

Behind the sappy romantic novels and sentimentality associated with love is a bred-in-the-bone longing. It is wired into our mammalian brain. This is why, even though we might get distracted into a one night sexual adventure, we still fight to connect and to hold onto our love relationships. Our most natural and longed for state is a strong, nurturing monogamous pair bond and on this bond we base our families.

The real issue here is that when we fail the monogamy test it is most often because we have no blueprint, no map for loving connection. Science now offers us such a map. Until very recently, we have not known what the bond of love, the basis of successful monogamy, is all about and how to shape it. Lets see how good monogamy can be now that we know how to love.

Reprinted with permission from www.holdmetight.com

Adam and Eve

by **Rabbi Joseph B. Soloveitchik**

Aloneness and Loneliness

With his emergence, man-*persona* encounters another problem of the human situation. Now, after man has been burdened with the ethical, halakhic norm and has become a metaphysical being – only now *Hashem Elokim* decides to create Eve, the woman. Prior to being commanded, man-*natura* led a non-reflective, outer-directed, instinctive existence in union with his nature.

Hence, he did not face the specific human problem by which *homo-persona* is troubled. Of course, we all know what the problem is; the Torah has revealed it. "It is not good that the man be *levaddo*" (Gen. 2:18). *Levaddo* has a twofold meaning: aloneness and loneliness. Man as a rule dislikes both; does not want to be alone; he hates to be lonely. We understand very well that to be alone and to be lonely are two different problems. One may stand at Times Square where hundreds of people pass by every minute and yet feel very lonely. Vice-versa, one may find oneself, in terms of distance, in seclusion, very remote from people, without feeling lonely.

To be alone is, first, a physical fact and, second, a psychological condition which is not at all universal. Some people are loners; they prefer to be with themselves without being intruded upon by others. Of course, at times this urge to be alone assumes abnormal proportions, as in the case of reclusion. However, to retreat from society and to spend time apart from people is a frequent and normal exercise. Many like being alone. Of course, usually man is (as Aristotle knew) a gregarious animal; the herd instinct is powerful. He does not like to shut off the World from his life and, if compelled to do so, he feels miserable. Man-*natura* as a rule hates aloneness.

However, loneliness is not a physical fact, nor is it a most painful psychological condition. It is far more than that. Loneliness is a spiritual human situation. If I may say, it is an existential awareness or a metaphysical state, not only of the mind but of the soul as well. Loneliness reflects both the greatness of man as a unique metaphysical being, as well as his ontological insecurity as an incomplete being who, like a trapped animal, searches for an exit from his labyrinthine existence. It is both an inspiring as well as destructive experience. Lonely man is both hero and coward, giant and dwarf. There is anxiety as well as joy in the loneliness situation. However, it is only man-*persona*— introspective, meditating, and experiencing estrangement from nature—who is lonely. Metaphysical man finds himself in the throes of loneliness. Man-*natura*, who leads a gregarious, complacent, ebullient non-metaphysical existence, is not acquainted with this situation.

Man-*natura* suffers from aloneness, never from loneliness. He is outer-oriented and success-minded, thinks scientifically, and is not conscious of another ontological order beside the natural one. In loneliness, humans long for bliss and beauty, for a higher and more meaningful order, purged of evil, redeemed from contradiction and absurdity.

Let us pick up the verse, "It is not good that the man be *levaddo*." We have asked, what did *Hashem Elokim* mean by this dictum, aloneness or loneliness, for *levaddo* lends itself to either interpretation. The answer to this question is, I believe, to be found in the laconic five-word original Hebrew sentence. The Torah could have said, "*lo tov la-adam lihyot levaddo*." However, it preferred the arrangement, "*lo tov heyot ha-adam levaddo*." What is the difference between these two formulations? The first would read, if translated into the vernacular, "It is not good for the man to be *levaddo*"; the second, "It is not good that the man be *levaddo*." The first, had it been used by the Bible, would have expressed a utilitarian rule. A man alone cannot accomplish as much as two. He needs a helper from a utilitarian viewpoint. The second formulation, which the Scripture actually uses, has a different connotation: man's being *levaddo* is not good. This is an ontological postulate. A lonely human existence is not good; it lacks God's sanction and exposes an imperfect form of being. The helper whom God willed to make is indispensable not only for a pragmatic but for an ontological reason as well. Man needs help ontologically. Another homo-*persona* is necessary to complete man's existence, to endow it with existential meaning and directedness.

Marriage is not just a successful partnership, but an existential community. Adam and Eve met and a new metaphysical community, not just a successful partnership, was born. Had Adam needed a partner for practical reasons alone—to lighten his economic burden, to enable him to procreate, or to allow him a satisfactory sexual life—there would have been no necessity for the creation of Eve. We know from reading the first chapter that God created male and female. Both were endowed with great skill, talent, know-how and technical aptitude to control their environment. Male and female could have formed a dynamic, profitable partnership or company which would efficiently take care of all human needs, be they economic, physiological, or psychological. There was no need for natural man to meet Eve the woman, since he was already in company of the female who, for all practical purposes, would have made an excellent wife.

However, something had happened to man. The rendezvous with *Hashem* which resulted in man's encounter with the moral norm precipitated the birth of *homo-persona*, of a metaphysical man, of a singular spiritual personality. New man was burdened with a new awareness, one of inadequacy, illegitimacy and rootlessness; he was troubled by a great anxiety, by a sickness unto death—fright. In a word, he found himself lonely and forsaken. What he needed was not a practical partnership but an ontological community where his lonely existence could find completeness and legitimacy. The female of the first chapter did not qualify for that type of a community. A new woman had to be created, a woman who, like man, changed from a natural into metaphysical being, from female-*natura* into woman-*persona*, into a unique spiritual personality.

What is actually the difference between homo-*natura* and homo-*persona*? What is the main feature of the *persona* of metaphysical man? The Torah gives the answer in the story about naming the animals. The story appears to destroy completely the unity and continuity of the tale about the creation of Eve. However, the last sentence sheds light upon the link between this story and the emergence of Eve. "And the man gave names to all cattle and to the fowl of the air and to every beast of the field, but for Adam there was not found a helpmate for him" (Gen. 2:20). The story about Adam giving names to all cattle and fowl revealed to man the distinction between what he was prior to the command and what he became following it.

Man's Otherness from Nature

Adam named all the living creatures. What kind of a performance was it, and why did God encourage him to do this? It was a cognitive gesture. Sciences are divided into descriptive sciences (such as general botany, general zoology, geography and even astronomy) and explanatory sciences (such as physics). The job of the descriptive scientist is to introduce order into an allegedly chaotic world, to classify and generalize—their question is *what*. The explanatory scientists are concerned not with the *what* but with the *how*: Their question is, *how* do those objects function? Their prime instrument of cognition is the category of causality.

God wanted Adam to inquire into the what-ness of the world from a descriptive viewpoint. He encouraged Adam to classify and systematize a motley world which, at first glance, impresses us with its disorderliness and disarray. Primitive man saw no patterns in nature; he considered the latter replete with contradictions. Man started his progress by first introducing order into his environment, by classifying the fauna (and perhaps also the flora). This is the first scientific approach to nature: no magic, no spirit indwelling in every bush, no Golden Bough. Objective Adam approached his environment scientifically and tried to introduce orderliness.

At this point, there takes place man's breach with absolute, all-inclusive natural immediacy and his acquisition of a new capacity, that of turning around and facing the environment as something external and strange. Man, in order to become the ruler and developer of nature, must make an about face. Instead of marching naively with nature, he must suddenly stop moving along and encounter nature with the first question: what is it? When he begins to wonder what nature is and tries to understand it, he abandons the identity and unity of man and his environment and finds himself encountering it as a stranger and outsider.

At this point man discovers in himself an incommensurability with nature. He enters into a new phase in his emergence as a person: he views nature not from within but from without. While watching nature at a distance he gradually moves into a unique position of power and specific rights. The creative urge in man frees him from the state of all-out integration into one's environment.

Thus man experiences both oneness with and otherness from nature. He is an exponent of his kind, a representative of the group whose claim to existence is justified only at a generic level, and he is also an individual, a separate entity, who exists because he is himself, without being placed in a generic frame of reference. When man reaches the stage at which he is no longer a non-reflective being that forges ahead in unison with a mechanical-natural occurrence, but instead begins to single himself out in an act of confrontation with nature, he suddenly discovers in himself his own intelligence. He faces nature in a cognitive, critical, observant mood. The creative drive in him awakens in him curiosity and the desire for inquiry. The inquiry about the how, what and why, the quest for creativity comes to expression. Man begins to survey his environment and to uncover certain functional patterns of behavior.

When man breaks with immediacy and takes a look at nature from a distance, he encounters a reality which is not only outside of himself but also opposed to him. He is required to venture into an alien sphere. Aware of himself as an autonomous being capable of making decisions and charting a course of action, he also knows that the implementation of his decision depends upon something else, upon something outside of himself which can thwart the whole project he has conceived and organized. He must act, because God has implanted in him the urge to activate himself, and yet, at the same time, he cannot act, because he is removed from his exalted position as a subject and demoted to a mere object who bears consequences and is immobilized by the impact of events and things not of his making.

While Adam was busy describing, a great truth dawned on him. He realized that knowledge of the surrounding world by observation is gained by watching how the objects attracting our attention function. Objective observation is the source of knowledge of the world. However when it comes to man, observation alone will yield a very meager amount of knowledge. Man must confide in the person who is eager to understand him. Without confession there can hardly be an opportunity to learn why, who, and what a particular individual is. In order for man to be recognized, he must reveal himself; he must be interrogated and interviewed. The person whom I am eager to know must have confidence in the investigator, and be willing to state everything he knows about himself sincerely and truthfully. And even then the knowledge will not be complete, since many things are hidden from the eye of the person himself.

There is no depth to nature. Its existence is a flat two-dimensional one. The reality of nature exhausts itself in its functions. If you ask whether mute nature exists, I shall certainly answer "of course." However, if you continue to cross-examine me and ask me what I understand by existence, I will answer "activity." The existence of nature exhausts itself in its behavior, in its dynamics. There is nothing else to a mute existence. Hence, by watching the behavioral patterns, I gain an insight into the substance. Nature does not lie.

However man has an inner world; he exists inwardly as well as externally. Man's ontological essence, that is, the essence of his being, is not to be equated with his conduct or routine activities. There is a *homo absconditus*, a "hidden man" whom no one knows. He hardly knows himself. Hence in spite of watching man's activity we gain little knowledge. The latter is a mystery which no one can unravel. "All men are liars," says the Psalmist (Psalms 116:11). Not because they want to tell the untruth. They are simply unable to tell the truth. I see my neighbor every morning leave his house at 6:30; I know to where he drives off. I am also familiar with his occupation. I know what he will do when he will arrive at his place of business. I willy-nilly watched his conduct; I am acquainted with his habits and responses to certain challenges. I overhear his conversation with the members of his household, I know his concerns and interests. Do I know *him*? No, he is a mystery to me. The uniqueness of man-*persona* expresses itself in the *mysterium magnum* which no one except God can penetrate.

In order to escape loneliness, man-*absconditus* had to meet woman-mystery. They have a lot in common; otherwise Eve could not be a helper. However, they are also different; their existential experiences are incommensurate. The I-awareness in Adam is totally incomprehensible to Eve, and vice-versa. Each of them has a secret which neither will ever betray. Man-*persona* and woman-*persona* resemble each other and at the same time do not understand each other. She is *ezer ke-negdo*, his helper and his opponent at the same time. For man and woman differ not only physiologically as male and female, of whom the first account of creation tells us, but also spiritually and personality-wise. This is the way in which the Creator has ordained human lonely destiny. Because the woman is not the shadow of man but an independent *persona*, because the woman projects a totally different existential image, her companionship helps man to liberate himself from his loneliness. In the interpersonalistic existential tension both man and woman find redemption.

Family Redeemed: Essays on Family Relationships
[Hoboken, NJ: Toras Horav Foundation, 2000], 15–22
Reprinted with permission of the publisher

Lesson 2
Bedroom Secrets
A Jewish View on Intimacy

Introduction

Though sexual intimacy probably wasn't broached by your Hebrew school teacher, Judaism has much to say on the topic. It is common knowledge that Judaism doesn't advocate celibacy, but many don't know that Judaism views sexual intimacy as sacred (and not only because of its procreative value), and even fewer people are aware that the Torah provides the perspective and practical tools to experience heightened passion and intimacy.

Is G-d Comfortable in the Bedroom?
Marriage: Holy or Profane?

Text 1

Celibacy has existed in one form or another throughout history and in virtually all the major religions of the world.

Encyclopædia Britannica Online, s. v. "celibacy," www. britannica.com/EBchecked/topic/101371/celibacy

Question for Discussion

Why does celibacy qualify as a generic spiritual and religious ideal?

Text 2

In a *religious* setting the obstacle the body imposes on one's mind would be conceptualized as a barrier between the individual and God. Therefore, to become closer to God mean[s] to become alienated from one's body and bodily functions—first and foremost from the sexual drive. As a result, the abstinence from sex was regarded by this intellectual and emotional stance as leading to a more perfect human state and to closeness to God.

Adiel Schremer, "Marriage, Sexuality, and Holiness: The Anti-Ascetic Legacy of Talmudic Judaism," in Rivkah Blau, ed., *Gender Relationships in Marriage and Out* [New York: Yeshiva University Press, 2007], p. 48

Adiel Schremer (1965–). Associate professor of Jewish history at Bar-Ilan University and head of the Halpern Center for the Study of Jewish Self-Perception. His publications include *Male and Female He Created Them* and *Brothers Estranged*.

Text 3

The chief cause of ignorance is the flesh and our affinity for it. Moses himself affirms this when he says [that] "because they are flesh," the divine spirit cannot abide. Marriage, indeed, and the rearing of children, the provision of necessities, the ill repute that comes in the wake of poverty, business both private and public, and a host of other things wilt the flower of wisdom before it blooms. Nothing, however, so thwarts its growth as our fleshly nature.

Philo of Alexandria, *The Contemplative Life, The Giants, and Selections* [New York: Paulist Press, 1981], p. 65

Philo of Alexandria (ca. 10 BCE–50 CE). A Jewish Hellenist philosopher who attempted to synthesize Jewish thought with Greek philosophy. He was a member of the delegation sent by Alexandrian Jewry to Emperor Caligula as the result of civil strife between the Jewish and hellenized communities of Alexandria. His works were important for several Christian church fathers, but for the most part, they have been ignored within traditional Judaism.

Where Heaven Meets Earth

Text 4a 📕

וְעָשִׂיתָ כַפֹּרֶת זָהָב טָהוֹר . . . וְעָשִׂיתָ שְׁנַיִם כְּרֻבִים זָהָב, מִקְשָׁה תַּעֲשֶׂה אֹתָם מִשְּׁנֵי קְצוֹת הַכַּפֹּרֶת . . . וְהָיוּ הַכְּרֻבִים פֹּרְשֵׂי כְנָפַיִם לְמַעְלָה סֹכְכִים בְּכַנְפֵיהֶם עַל הַכַּפֹּרֶת וּפְנֵיהֶם אִישׁ אֶל אָחִיו.

שמות כה,יז-כ

And you shall make an ark cover of pure gold. . . . And you shall make two golden cherubim of hammered work, [rising] from the two ends of the ark cover. . . . The cherubim shall have their wings spread upwards, shielding the ark cover with their wings, with their faces toward one another.

Exodus 25:17–20

Text 4b 📘

וְנוֹעַדְתִּי לְךָ שָׁם וְדִבַּרְתִּי אִתְּךָ מֵעַל הַכַּפֹּרֶת מִבֵּין שְׁנֵי הַכְּרֻבִים אֲשֶׁר עַל אֲרֹן הָעֵדֻת אֵת כָּל אֲשֶׁר אֲצַוֶּה אוֹתְךָ אֶל בְּנֵי יִשְׂרָאֵל.

שם כה,כב

I will arrange My meetings with you there; from atop the ark's cover, from between the two cherubim that are upon the ark of the testimony, I will tell you all that I will instruct you [to relay to] the Children of Israel.

Ibid., 25:22

Text 5 📖

בשעה שהיו ישראל עולין לרגל, מגללין להם את הפרוכת ומראין להם את הכרובים שהיו מעורים זה בזה, ואומרים להן: "ראו חבתכם לפני המקום כחבת זכר ונקבה".

תלמוד בבלי, יומא נד,א

When the Jewish people came up to [Jerusalem for] the festivals, the curtain [that was in front of the Holy of Holies] was rolled aside, and the cherubim—whose bodies were intertwined one with another—were shown to to them. And the [assembled Jews] were told: "Look! You are beloved before God as the love between man and woman."

Talmud, Yoma 54a

Babylonian Talmud. A literary work of monumental proportions that draws upon the totality of the legal, spiritual, intellectual, ethical, and historical traditions of Judaism, the Babylonian Talmud was set up as a commentary to the Mishnah and was written primarily in Aramaic. The Talmud contains the teachings of the Jewish sages, mostly from the period after the destruction of the Second Temple through the fifth century C.E. The Babylonian Talmud has served as the primary vehicle for the education of countless Jews over the centuries; it is the entry point for all subsequent legal, ethical, and theological Jewish scholarship.

Text 6a 📖

בשעה שנכנסו נכרים להיכל ראו כרובים המעורין זה בזה. הוציאון לשוק ואמרו, "ישראל הללו . . . יעסקו בדברים הללו?" מיד הזילום, שנאמר (איכה א,ח), "כל מכבדיה הזילוה כי ראו ערותה".

שם, נד,ב

When the heathens entered the Temple and saw the cherubim, whose bodies were intertwined with one another, they carried them out to the marketplace and said: "These Jews . . . preoccupy themselves with such things!" Immediately, all who saw this display despised the Jews, as it is said (Lamentations 1:8): "All who honored her now scorned her, because they saw her disgrace."

Talmud, ibid., 54b

Text 6b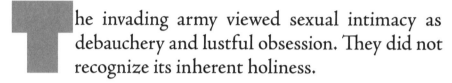

דאצלם נחשב זה ערוה ושיקוע תאוה, כי הם אינם יודעים שיש מציאות קדושה בענין זה.

קדושת שבת, מאמר ו

Rabbi Tsadok Hakohen Rabinowitz of Lublin (1823-1900). Chasidic rebbe and prolific author. Born to a Lithuanian rabbinic family, as a young man he became a follower of Rabbi Mordechai Yosef Leiner of Izhbitsa. He authored many works on Jewish law, Chasidism, Kabbalah, and ethics, as well as scholarly essays on astronomy, geometry, and algebra. He is buried in Lublin.

The invading army viewed sexual intimacy as debauchery and lustful obsession. They did not recognize its inherent holiness.

Rabbi Tsadok Hakohen Rabinowitz, *Kedushat Shabbat, Ma'amar 6*

Text 6c

הנה החיבור הוא ענין עלוי גדול כשיהיה כפי הראוי, והסוד הגדול הזה סוד גדול בכרובים שהיו מעורים זה בזה בדמיון זכר ונקבה.

ואילו היה בדבר גנאי, לא היה מצוה רבונו של עולם לעשות ככה ולשום אותם במקום היותר קדוש וטהור שבכל הישוב.

אגרת הקודש להרמב״ן, פרק ב

Rabbi Moshe ben Nachman (1194–1270). Also known as Nachmanides, or by the acronym Ramban; born in Spain, he served as leader of Iberian Jewry. Nachmanides authored a classic commentary on the Pentateuch that includes everything from critical examination of the text to kabbalistic insights. He also authored numerous other works, including a commentary on the Talmud. In 1263, he was summoned by King James of Aragon to a public disputation with Pablo Cristiani, a Jewish apostate. Though he was the clear victor of the debate, resulting persecution led to his expulsion from Spain. Settling in Israel, Nachmanides helped reestablish communal life in Jerusalem.

Intimacy, when properly experienced, is great and sublime. It shares the profound secret of the cherubim, which were in the form of a male and female intertwined with one another.

If sexual intimacy were shameful, God would not have commanded to fashion the cherubim and place them in the holiest and purest place in the world!

Rabbi Moshe ben Nachman, *Igeret Hakodesh 2*

The Human Cherubim

Text 7a

אִישׁ וְאִשָּׁה, זָכוּ, שְׁכִינָה בֵּינֵיהֶן.

תלמוד בבלי, סוטה יז,א

When a husband and wife are worthy, God resides between them.

Talmud, Sotah 17a

Text 7b

שֶׁהֲרֵי חָלַק אֶת שְׁמוֹ וְשִׁכְּנוֹ בֵּינֵיהֶן—יו"ד בְּאִישׁ, וה"י בְּאִשָּׁה.

רש"י, שם

For God divided His name between them— a *yud* in the man, and a *hei* in the woman.

Rashi, ad loc.

Figure 2.1

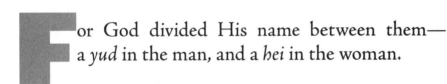

Rabbi Shlomo Yitschaki (1040–1105). Better known by the acronym Rashi. Rabbi and famed author of comprehensive commentaries on the Talmud and Bible. Born in Troyes, France, Rashi studied in the famed *yeshivot* of Mainz and Worms. His commentaries, which focus on the simple understanding of the text, are considered the most fundamental of all commentaries. Since their initial printings, the commentaries have appeared in virtually every edition of the Talmud and Bible. Many of the famed authors of the *Tosafot* are among Rashi's descendants.

Text 7c

Rabbi Yehudah Loew (1525–1609). Talmudist and philosopher, also known as the Maharal of Prague. Descended from the Babylonian exilarchs, Maharal rose to prominence as leader of the famed Jewish community of Prague. He is the author of more than a dozen works of original philosophic thought, most notably *Tiferet Yisrael* and *Netsach Yisrael*. He also authored a commentary on the Talmud, and *Gur Aryeh*, a super-commentary on Rashi's biblical commentary. He is buried in the Old Jewish Cemetery of Prague.

כי איש ואשה שכל אחד מהם חלק האדם, ושניהם ביחד הם אדם שלם. ולפי מעלת האדם כאשר הוא שלם השכינה עמו, כי השם יתברך שמו חל על כל דבר שלם. וכך כאשר יתחברו יחד והם אדם שלם, שמו יתברך חל עליהם.

חידושי אגדות מהר"ל, שם

The degree of God's presence in a person's life depends on the degree of his or her perfection. Man and woman are individually incomplete; together, they constitute a complete and perfected being. Thus, when man and woman unite, God rests upon them.

Rabbi Yehudah Loew, *Chidushei Agadot*, ad loc.

Text 8

כתיב (איוב כג,יג), "והוא באחד . . .".

לא שארי קודשא בריך הוא ולא אשתכח אלא באחד. "באחד"? "אחד" מבעי ליה!
אלא במאן דאתתקן בקדושה עלאה למהוי חד, כדין הוא שריא באחד ולא באתר אחרא.
ואימתי אקרי בר נש אחד . . . בזמנא דאשתכח בר נש בזווגא . . . וכד מתחברן דכר
ונוקבא כדין אתעבידו חד גופא, אשתכח דאינהו חד נפשא וחד גופא ואקרי בר נש
אחד, כדין קודשא בריך הוא שארי הוא באחד.

זוהר ג, פ,א–ב

It is written (Job 23:13): "He is in one. . . ."

"[He is] *in* one"? Should it not read, "[He] *is* one"?
[The meaning of this verse is that] God only
abides and dwells "in one," in the person who achieves a
holy oneness—nowhere else.

When is a person called "one"? . . . When a person is in
the union of intimacy. . . . When male and female join,
they become one. They are one in body and one in soul;
they are one person. And God dwells in the oneness.

Zohar 3:80a–b

Zohar. The most seminal work of Kabbalah, Jewish mysticism. It is a mystical commentary on the Torah, written in Aramaic and Hebrew. According to Arizal, the Zohar consists of the teachings of Rabbi Shimon bar Yocha'i who lived in the Land of Israel during the 2nd century. The Zohar has become one of the indispensable texts of traditional Judaism, alongside and nearly equal in stature to the Mishnah and Talmud.

Intimacy on Three Levels
Unity and Holiness

Figure 2.2

Level One: Containment

Text 9

אבר קטן יש לו לאדם, מרעיבו—שבע, משביעו—רעב.

תלמוד בבלי, סוכה נב,ב

Man possesses a small organ: if starved, it is satiated; if satiated, it hungers.

Talmud, Sukah 52b

Question **for Discussion**

In view of Judaism's anti-abstinence stance, what is the meaning of this Talmudic passage?

Optional Section

Questions **for Discussion**

What are the common threads that bind the rules and recommendations we discussed? Moreover, why curtail natural expression? Can't people just "be themselves" during these deeply personal moments?

End of Optional Section

Level Two: Responsiveness

Text 10a

שְׁאֵרָהּ כְּסוּתָהּ וְעֹנָתָהּ לֹא יִגְרָע.

שמות כא,י

A husband must fully provide for his wife's food, clothing, and conjugal needs.

Exodus 21:10

Text 10b

ועונתה מלשון "עונה", שזה מענה על שאלת הטבע.

משך חכמה, שם

Rabbi Meir Simcha Hakohen of Dvinsk (1843–1926). Served as rabbi of Dvinsk for nearly 40 years. In 1906, he was offered the position of rabbi of Jerusalem but bowed to the entreaties of the city folk to remain in Dvinsk. He is renowned for two works: *Or Same'ach*, a commentary on Maimonides' *Mishneh Torah,* and *Meshech Chochmah*, a profound commentary on the Bible. In the latter work, Rabbi Meir Simcha demonstrates the compatibility of the Written and Oral Laws and presents original interpretations of biblical and Talmudic passages.

Onatah is linguistically related to the word *oneh* (to respond), for this mitzvah [requires the husband] to respond to [his wife's] natural needs.

Rabbi Meir Simcha Hakohen of Dvinsk, *Meshech Chochmah*, ad loc.

Level Three: Procreation

Text 11a

וַיְבָרֶךְ אֹתָם אֱלֹקִים וַיֹּאמֶר לָהֶם אֱלֹקִים, "פְּרוּ וּרְבוּ".

ברא שית א,כח

And God blessed them, and God said to them: "Be fruitful and multiply."

Genesis 1:28

Text 11b

תולדותיו של אדם, אלו מעשיו הטובים.

מדרש תנחומא, נח ב

A person's progeny are his or her good deeds.

Midrash Tanchuma, Noach 2

Midrash Tanchuma is an early rabbinic commentary on the Pentateuch bearing the name of Rabbi Tanchuma, a 4th-century Talmudic sage who is often quoted in this work. This *midrash* provides textual exegeses and stories, expounds upon the biblical narrative, and develops and illustrates moral principles. *Tanchuma* is unique in that many of its sections commence with a halachic question and answer that subsequently leads into the non-legal teachings.

Text 11c

Rabbi Menachem Mendel Schneerson (1902–1994). Known as "the Lubavitcher Rebbe," or simply as "the Rebbe." Born in southern Ukraine, Rabbi Schneerson escaped Nazi-occupied Europe, arriving in the U.S. in June 1941. The towering Jewish leader of the 20th century, the Rebbe inspired and guided the revival of traditional Judaism after the European devastation, impacting virtually every Jewish community the world over. The Rebbe often emphasized that the performance of just one additional good deed could usher in the era of Mashiach. The Rebbe's scholarly talks and writings have been printed in more than 200 volumes.

The mitzvah to "be fruitful and multiply" is intended not only physically, but also spiritually.

There is a chasidic aphorism explaining why procreation is the first mitzvah in the Torah: "The order in which Torah conveys its messages is also instructive. The first principle of Jewish life is, 'One Jew must create another Jew.'"

The Lubavitcher Rebbe, Rabbi Menachem Mendel Schneerson, *Likutei Sichot* 1:114

Text 12a

וַיְהִי בָרָד, וְאֵשׁ מִתְלַקַּחַת בְּתוֹךְ הַבָּרָד.

שמות ט,כד

There was hail, and fire blazed within the hail.

Exodus 9:24

Text 12b

האש והברד מעורבין, והברד מים הוא, ולעשות רצון קונם עשו שלום ביניהם.

רש"י, שם

Fire was mixed with the hail. Though hail is [frozen] water, the fire and water made peace in order to do the will of their Creator.

Rashi, ad loc.

Don't have to do all at once

Text 13

הולד נוצר על ידי שניהם, ושם נעשה בשרם אחד.

רש"י, בראשית ב,כד

The child is formed by them both, and [in the child] they become one flesh. *the ultimate*

Rashi, Genesis 2:24

Worlds of Intimacy

Optional Section

Text 14

Rabbi Chaim Vital (1542–1620). Born in Israel, lived in Safed, Jerusalem, and later Damascus. Vital was the principal disciple of Arizal, though he studied under him for less than two years. Before his passing, Arizal authorized Vital to record his teachings. Acting on this mandate, Vital began arranging his master's teachings in written form, and his many works constitute the foundation of the Lurianic school of Jewish mysticism, which was later universally adopted as the kabbalistic standard. Thus, Vital is one of the most important influences in the development of Kabbalah. Among his most famous works are *Ets Chayim*, and *Sha'ar Hakavanot*.

בעולם אצילות של הקדושה, הטוב מרובה... ואינם מעורבים כלל הקדושה עם הטומאה.

ובעולם הבריאה, הקדושה מרובה על הטומאה...

וביצירה, הוא מחצה על מחצה...

ובעשיה, הקליפה מרובה על העשיה של טהרה.

עץ חיים מח,ג

In the holy realm of *Atsilut,* good is abundant . . . and there is no blending of unholiness with holiness.

In the realm of *Beri'ah,* holiness overshadows unholiness. . . .

In *Yetsirah,* [holiness and unholiness] are evenly divided. . . .

In *Asiyah,* unholiness overshadows holiness.

Rabbi Chaim Vital, *Ets Chayim* 48:3

End of Optional Section

Key Points

1. In contrast to many religions, Judaism does not endorse celibacy. In fact, it views intimacy between husband and wife as holy.

2. The love between husband and wife is God's abode of choice.

3. The presence of God in a marriage correlates to the level of unity achieved by the couple. This unity is reached when each spouse transcends his or her own self-serving needs in favor of focusing on the other.

4. The apex of holiness is reached at the time of intimacy—the moment when the couple reaches the ultimate unity of mind, heart, body, and soul.

5. Intimacy is a potent force and must therefore be harnessed and properly channeled. The Torah's guidelines surrounding intimacy are designed to ensure that the couple is able to minimize distractions, focus on each other, and tap into the awesome power of intimacy.

6. By mandating intimacy at regular intervals, the Torah ensures that the man is responsive to the woman's needs and vice versa.

7. A Jewish marriage benefits society by bringing Jewish children into the world. When husband and wife are both committed to the same ideal—creating physical and/or spiritual offspring—they become "one flesh," both in a spiritual sense and physically through the creation of a child.

Additional Readings

"Full Frontal Feminism": The False Front

by **Chava Shapiro**

In one of my classes during my freshman year of college, the professor assigned a chapter from the book *Full Frontal Feminism: A Young Woman's Guide to Why Feminism Matters*. The chapter was titled, "Feminists Do it Better (And Other Sex Tips)." The basic idea: Once you get past all of the anti-sex nonsense that these religious right-wing maniacs are propagating, you'll be liberated, empowered and, subsequently, "great in bed."

The author begins by debunking the apparent myth that feminists are opposed to sex. ("I'm better in bed than you are," she begins, "and I have feminism to thank for it.") She goes on to explain that, while they represent two extremes of the spectrum, "abstinence-only education during the day and Girls Gone Wild commercials at night" essentially promote the same idea—that women can't make their own decisions about sex. Armed with this premise, she concludes that whether by telling girls that sex is sinful or by exploiting their bodies for entertainment, our society conspires to make sure that women don't "have a good time in bed."

Hold on. Rewind. Yes, we must reject the abstinence-only education model that tells young women they are worthless without their virginity. Yes, we must reject the Girls Gone Wild mentality that treats women's bodies like commodities. But where did this conclusion come from, this assertion that all we girls really want is to have fun (I'll forgo the song reference)? Obviously, women want to be intimate without feeling guilty, sinful, debased, or dehumanized . . . But for fun? Roller coasters are fun. Live concerts are fun. Water-skiing is fun. Far from empowering, the Sex-for-Fun campaign turns intimacy into something cheap, shallow, empty and entirely degrading.

Of course, the sexual revolution is not a novel idea but an implacably entrenched one. Many young women today feel pressured by the societal expectation to have casual sex in much the same way that their mothers felt pressured by the societal expectation to stay a virgin until marriage. In fact, young girls are often treated as somewhat pathological for wanting to wait until marriage. Unfortunately, many parents actually add to the pressure by stressing their understanding of the inner-workings of the modern teenage relationship, justifying their passivity by shrugging and saying, "Well, they're gonna do it anyway." This idea that sex is "no big deal" is depressing and, frankly, dangerous. And not just because of STDs. Study after study shows that the more sexual experience that girls have as teenagers, the more prone they are to depression and suicide.

Yet there are also dangerous consequences of telling girls that sex is inherently sinful and that they are worthless without their virginity. Making girls feel shamed and punished doesn't exactly promote a healthy body image and self-esteem. This approach even has the opposite effect often times, leading girls to rebel violently against what they see as oppressive abstinence-only propaganda.

Sex is the single most powerful and pervasive force in human existence. As a Jewish woman, I am fascinated with the extent to which Judaism outright rejects the mainstream Christian view of sex as a sinful and shameful act. Even in the context of marriage, Christianity sees sex as a necessary compromise, mainly to prevent humanity from dying out. (Meaning, you're not necessarily going to hell, but it's far from the ideal.) Furthermore, most religions view sex as taboo, while there are pages and pages of Talmud throughout which our sages discuss intimacy in intricate detail, down to the nitty-gritty. These teachings go back over 1,500 years.

In most religions, asceticism is the ultimate path to spirituality, but Judaism teaches that divorcing ourselves from the physical world actually goes against our mission, which is to make this world a place for Godliness; only through engaging with the physical can we access the divine. So, it makes sense that Judaism teaches that through intimacy, the single-most physical human act, one can reach the height of holiness. Importantly, while this largely stems from the potential to create human life, the holiness of intimacy is not dependent on the possibility or intention for procreation. The relationship between a Jewish husband and wife is, in itself, sacred.

Yet the powerful nature of intimacy is most evident in the fact that, depending on its context, it can give one a taste of the highest of spiritual heights or the lowest spiritual depths. Intimacy can be a meaningful, uplifting, intensely personal experience or a depersonalized, careless, purely biological release. Sex is the most chaotic and unrestrained of human instincts, but its beauty is experienced most completely in the confines of discipline and precision. It's a remarkable paradox.

We live in a narcissistic world, a world obsessed with immediate pleasure and instant gratification. So much of what we do is intended to feed our egotistical, animalistic drives. But young women don't need to do too much self-searching in order to realize that we instinctively need meaning, love and commitment in relationships. It's just how we're wired, and no so-called feminist can convince us that being shallow pleasure-seekers is somehow liberating. It's time we start embracing real relationships and rejecting sex as a recreational sport. It's time we reclaim the true meaning of sexual liberation. It's time we start a new revolution.

Printed with permission of the author

The Sexual Component in Love and Marriage

by **Rabbi Maurice Lamm**

The Power of Sex

Sex is the most powerful, all-pervasive force in human experience. It may be intensely personal, meaningful, and creative at one moment, and depersonalized, meaningless, and careless the next. Much of its glory is that it can bring us as close as we may get in life to experiencing the mystery of our mortality, and because of this it is sanctified. Yet it can also be a blind, nearly irresistible force seeking wanton release on the biological level, and in this way its sanctity is perverted. Paradoxically, sex—the most chaotic, powerful, and untutored drive—can only be fully experienced when it includes an element of discipline and precision.

Theologian Helmut Thielicke postulates a theology of sex on the premise that not even an iron will can truly withstand its force. *En apotropus le arayot*, the Talmud teaches: "No one can guarantee another's sexual innocence." Long ago the Rabbis said, "The greater the man, the greater the desire," equating personal power and libidinal power. "The sexual attraction first engages the eyes," say the moralists, "and the only effective way to eliminate immorality is to avoid its grasp at every turn."

But temptation, in the form of magazines, books, and movies, is a multi-billion dollar industry and permeates our society. The abuse of human sexuality has reached the stomach-turning point, and there seems to be no way to avoid it—no exertion of universal wills, no permanent cover for the eyes. It is ironic that this situation should exist at a time when cults are multiplying, more people are praying, and atheists are being ridiculed into extinction. It seems we are at a time of religious boom and moral bust.

You may ask, "What else is new?" Haven't religious and ethical leaders throughout history decried society's lack of morality? Yes, but it is different today. Not because the sanctity of sex is violated in practice, not because television brings temptation into the family's inner sanctum, and not because sexual gratification is readily available. Today sexual morality is rejected as an ideal, modesty is scoffed at, and chastity is rejected as anachronistic. Worse, those who articulately uphold moral standards, modesty, and chastity are disappearing; their arguments appear irrelevant.

The Bible rejects one who does only "whatsoever is right in his own eyes" (Deuteronomy 12:8). Today, the philosophy that "man is the measure of all things" is not confined to one group, it is the heritage of our whole society. If we are to be the final arbiters of all value, it follows that whatever serves our needs is declared "good." "The good life" is a life devoted to sensual experience—tennis, water-skiing, the theater. These activities are not intrinsically wrong; but it is noteworthy that the most basic ethical term is so easily transferred to physical pleasure.

We have adopted an ideology of narcissism informed by situational ethics: if you have pleasure and mutual consent anything goes—as long as no one gets hurt. For example, what is disturbing is not the ethical merit of a particular abortion, but the rationale for wholesale abortions: "It's my body and I can do what I want with it." Similarly, there is hardly a trace of guilt to be found in those responsible for media presentations of what is now considered "old-fashioned" sexual immorality. No attempt is made to correct the situation—that's just the way it is. But worse is the accepted justification for casual sex or an adulterous affair: "It makes me happy."

Today contraception, not conception, is the focus of research. The sex act has effectively been separated from its fulfillment—one is play, the other pro-creation. In a day when coitus is no longer necessarily connected with reproduction or with responsibility, not many pregnancies are likely to survive both contraception and abortion.

Today there is no talk of standards, G-d's or society's. It seems sex is all right in every form—so long as it is not repressed, Freud forbid. We are faced with this question: What shall sex be used for now that it is no longer tied to that sacred, cosmically significant function of perpetuating the family, the faith, and the human race?

Society's answer appears to be very simple: fun—and fun has no rules.

Judaism on Sexual Boundaries

There is no single term for "sex" in the Bible. The title for the list of the Bible's prohibited sexual offenses is *gilui arayot*, "uncovering the nakedness" (Leviticus 18:6ff), and Maimonides classifies these chapters of the law under the rubric of *Kedushah* (Sanctity). Although Jewish tradition does not treat sexual experience systematically, reference to it can be found in every one of the Five Books of Moses, in every book of the Prophets, and *Ketuvim*, the "Writings." Even the Talmud contains candid, sometimes explicit clinical analyses and intimate details that would make a Victorian blush. What emerges is a moral discipline that is strict, yet highly sensitive to the human condition; one that affirms the joyfulness of the sexual experience, but insists that it express itself in controlled circumstances; and one that never deprecates marriage and at every opportunity deplores monastic asceticism.

Judaism's philosophy of sexual experience, love, and marriage begins with the Bible's first recorded paragraphs describing Adam's relations with Eve. This philosophy has weathered every new fad and every radical style that boldly declared its doctrine to the world, from the celibacy of Augustine to the free love of Bertrand Russell. Judaism has focused its greatest minds on understanding G-d's law and nature's demands, and throughout its history has succeeded in elevating sex, sanctifying marriage, and firmly establishing the family as the primary unit of the community.

Traditional Judaism makes the following general propositions about sex and its place in human society:

1. Sexual relations may take place only between a man and a woman. This means that sex with an animal is considered a perversion, and intercourse with a member of one's own sex prohibited.

2. Sexual relations and marriage are not permitted with someone outside the circle of the Jewish people (mixed marriage) or inside the circle of close relatives established by the Bible and the Sages (incest).

3. Sexual relations are a *mitzvah*, a religious duty, within a properly covenanted marriage in accordance with Jewish law. Outside of that covenant, premarital sexual relations are not condoned and extramarital relations are considered crimes.

4. Sexual relations within marriage must accord with the laws of family purity with respect to the wife's menstrual cycle.

Rabbi Akiva deduced these fundamental ideas from a single verse (Genesis 2:24): "Therefore shall a man leave his father and his mother and shall cleave unto his wife, and they shall be one flesh." By extension, "his father" also includes his father's wife, even if she is not his mother, and his "mother" is meant literally—to exclude incest. "And he shall cleave," but not to another male—to exclude homosexuality; "to his wife," not to his neighbor's wife—to exclude adultery; "And they shall be as one flesh," not to animals—to exclude buggery.

Seven Axioms for Sexual Conduct

These propositions are based largely on the following axioms that form the fundamental concepts of human sexuality in Judaism.

1. The Human Being Is Not an Animal

Simple observation teaches us that we have the genitalia of animals and participate in a similar sexual process. Why, then, can we not act like animals? It does seem to be nature's way. Indeed, Freudian psychology teaches us generally that we must see ourselves as we are, pleasure-seeking animals, and that we will not succeed in negating our essential animality except at the risk of neurosis. In the physical and psychological sense, then, human beings are considered to be fundamentally no more than animals.

Convinced of the truth of this specious reductionism—that we are nothing but animals—we begin to act that way without guilt, and even with gusto. There are no rules for beasts to follow other than blind obedience to instincts, satisfaction of needs, and "doing what comes naturally." The consequences of this irresponsible behavior can be disastrous, resulting in broken homes, broken hearts, loneliness, children born out of wedlock, loveless marriages, and infidelity. Ecclesiastes (3:19) declares only in bitterness, "Man has no preeminence above a beast, for all is vanity." But if that is all we are, then the world, humanity, the soul, and all of life becomes meaningless and empty. We were created in the image of G-d, and Judaism does not permit us to squander our humanity. *Ha-neshamah lakh ve'ha-guf Pa'alakh* ("the soul is Yours [G-d's] and the body is Yours, too") is a cornerstone phrase of the *Yom Kippur* liturgy. At the wedding service, a blessing is recited to remind the bride and groom that the human being is created in G-d's image.

Despite the similarity of sexual anatomy and parallel reproductive processes, the essential humanity of our sexuality can be discerned in the very fabric of the physical act. If it is to be successful, the sexual act must be based on a sense of concern for the partner. Helmut Thielicke notes that "there is a two-way communication in the structure of the libido, for the prerequisite for the fulfillment of pleasure is that the other person gives himself to it, that he participates. . . . The other person should not be a passive object upon which one's own urge is simply 'abreacted.'" Without this communication, coitus is disguised autoeroticism. We cannot successfully follow the animal instinct and achieve release, but must be synchronized with our partner in order to satisfy ourselves.

This "synchrony" required of sexual partners reflects a unique factor that is fundamental to our understanding of the difference between animal sex and human sex: A man's curve of sexual excitement tends to rise sharply and fall precipitously, while a woman's may rise more slowly and taper off gradually. At first this may appear to be an imperfection, when compared to the easy harmony of animals. But perhaps this apparent incongruity is designed to prevent human beings from merely following the erotic impulse in blind animal fashion. To achieve genuine satisfaction, we are forced to express our humanity. Sex exposes us to failure and success, and in all this it confronts us with the theme of human communication instead of mere animal copulation. It is precisely this human need to correct the natural impulse that impels the thirteenth-century author of *Iggeret ha-Kodesh*, a document on the mystical significance of marriage, to give detailed advice to his son on preparing his wife for the sexual act and designing the proper erotic atmosphere.

This exception of the human being from the rule of instinct in the natural realm teaches us that we must exercise our essential humanity in the area of sexual relations as in all other critical areas of life. We must reasonably and intelligently choose a life partner, make proper human covenants, order our lives and our priorities, control our urges, and submit to a higher discipline: a *halakhah*, the law we were given by G-d. This is a law that we need in order to protect our love, both from other humans who act like animals, and from the internal animal that we sometimes allow to crouch at the door of our souls.

While some segments of society attempt to animalize our humanity, Judaism tries to humanize that which is called animal.

If we are not animals—and thus not permitted to abuse our sexual gift—we are also not angels who may abstain from sex altogether. We must live according to a higher ethical and moral law as beings created in the image of G-d, but reality dictates that we are not, and will never become, angels.

Judaism therefore frowns on celibacy. As recorded in the Talmud, Ben Azzai (one scholar among the thousands recorded) chose to remain celibate in order to study Torah and was chastised severely. This is in stark contrast to the celibacy of the two founders of Christianity, Jesus and Paul, and the pronouncements against the institution of marriage (I Corinthians 6 and 7), which accept it only as a concession to human frailty. To wit, Paul: People should marry only " . . . if they cannot contain . . .; for it is better to marry than to burn" (I Cor. 7:9); and Matthew: "Be a eunuch for the sake of Heaven" (19:12); and John Calvin, at the beginning of the Protestant Reformation: Marriage is "a necessary remedy to keep us from plunging into unbridled lust." Reinhold Niebuhr considers the Christian development of the family a triumph over the negative Christian attitude to sex and marriage.

Judaism posits that sex is a gift from G-d. How could such a gift be considered evil or sinful? Properly used

in a legitimate framework, sex is to be viewed positively as joy and as *mitzvah*. The patriarchs marry, the kings marry, the *kohanim* marry, the prophets marry, and the Sages marry. Nowhere is there the slightest indication that sex or family interfered with their mission. The term used for Isaac's sexual relationship with his wife is *me'tzachek*, rejoicing (Genesis 26:8). The author of *Iggeret ha-Kodesh* writes: "Let a man not consider sexual union as something ugly or repulsive, for thereby we blaspheme G-d. Hands which write a Torah scroll are exalted and praiseworthy; hands which steal are ugly."

While the sexual act is considered good in the proper context, there were some ascetic pietists who viewed the sheer pleasure of even the legitimate act with some disdain. In the seventeenth century, Rabbi Hayyim Vital established the rule of Kabbalists: "He should sanctify himself at the time of intercourse so that he should derive no pleasure from it." However, the Seer of Lublin indicated that this applies before the act, as it is impossible to have no pleasure during the act. The Seer quotes Rabbi Elimelech of Lyzhansk, active in the eighteenth century, as saying that there is no benediction before performing the *mitzvah* of intercourse, "because it cannot be performed without an admixture of the 'evil' inclination." Nonetheless, while one should not seek pleasure from it, and while a full blessing may not be recited over it, the author concludes that we should thank G-d if we have received pleasure, so that we should not be guilty of using sacred things without proper acknowledgement.

Sex is not sin, and it does not need to be spiritualized. It must, however, be humanized, by affirming the reality of its power and attractiveness, rejoicing in its presence, using it as a blessing for the benefit and development of humankind, and abstaining from it when its Creator forbids it. A corollary of the two statements—that we are neither animals nor angels—may be that we have aspects of both. In this case, our humanity would consist of proper resolution of the tensions and contradictory demands made upon us by our dual nature.

3. Human Sexuality Is Clean and Neutral.

Judaism believes that sex is morally neutral. Libidinal energy is an ambivalent power, the effect of which depends on what the human being does with it. Sex does not even have the status of an intrinsic value, but can function as a means to express love and build family, or as random personal gratification. Sex is neither bestial nor sinful, neither sacrament nor abomination, and so may not be abused or discarded. It is not to be denigrated as a necessary concession to human weakness, nor is it to be worshipped as an idol.

Genesis (1:31) tells us that at the end of the creation, G-d saw everything that He made and that it was *tov me'od* (very good). Interpreting the verse, Rabbi Samuel ben Nahman said: "*Tov*, good—that is the *yetzer tov*, the good inclination; *tov me'od*, very good—that is the *yetzer ha-ra*, the evil inclination. But how can an admittedly evil inclination be considered good, let alone very good? Because without it, man would not care to build a home, he would neither marry nor beget children, nor would he pursue a livelihood."

Judaism does not believe that sex in itself is evil; it is the abuse of sex that is evil.

4. Sexuality Cannot Be Separated from Character.

If we agree that the sexual force is neutral and that its good or evil qualities depend on how we use it, we can begin to appreciate that our sexuality can never be separated from our total personality. Thus the way we handle our own sexuality is not primarily a matter of facts, but of values. Indeed, sex can be a revealing indication of character—is our partner a giver or taker, sensitive or gross, caring or selfish, religious or irreligious?

If sex were merely a matter of physiological function, it could be treated like a mechanical problem—get the best engine, use the best technique, and achieve the best result. If it doesn't work, trade it in. If this were the case, then sexual partners would be interchangeable, and society would function as a warehouse for suitable parts. This mechanical concept is analogous to prostitution, which is concerned solely with the biological function. It follows, therefore, that the more one's life is motivated by isolated instinct, the more one tends to polygamy and the less one seeks a single person with whom to share everlasting love.

The Jewish world view makes it clear that sex cannot be mechanically abstracted from the totality of human activity. Thus, the problems of premarital sex, adultery, and casual sex are really questions of values.

5. Human Sexuality Has Meaning Only in the Context of Relationship.

Perhaps our greatest fear is that our lives will be meaningless. If sex, the most powerful and sensitive area of our lives is to have meaning, it must be used as an expression of love or affection for another person. If we depersonalize the act by relating to another person only on a biological level, we dehumanize our partner and rob ourselves of our own integrity. To be successful, the act of sex requires the sensitive involvement of both partners. Noninvolvement results in a mechanical orgasm that is ultimately meaningless and demeaning.

If simply sleeping together would produce happiness, then the prostitute would be the happiest person in society. According to Helmut Thielicke, what is an ethical deficiency for the person who seeks the prostitute—the need for the physiological function rather than the person—is for the prostitute a positive element of moral self-defense. She saves her sense of self-worth by withholding her "self" during sex.

It is this distinction that determines whether the act is merely another sensation, or a true step toward relationship. It is becoming characteristic of our society that old as well as young people seek experiences rather than relationships, episodes rather than the continuous growth toward greater love. Ramban, in his commentary to the fundamental verse of love and marriage in Genesis (2:24), notes: "First one must cleave to his wife, and then they will become one flesh. There can be no true oneness of the flesh without first experiencing a cleaving together of the heart."

The later Rabbis analyze the specific commandment of *onah*, the *mitzvah* that requires the husband to care for his wife's conjugal needs. They ask whether the *mitzvah* requires only the object of the act (*cheftzah*), or the subjective involvement of the person in the performance (*gavra*). After finely dissecting the *mitzvah* and reducing it to its several legal components, they firmly maintain that the sex act ordained by the Bible as the right of the wife must be accompanied by closeness (*kiruv*), and joy (*simchah*). Both of these qualities require *gavra*, the involvement of the total personality, not merely a physical performance.

The sexual union of two people on a primitive, impersonal, casual, biological level is a gross misfortune. If it is by mutual consent, it is simply mutual exploitation. It has met the test of liberty in that it is not coerced, but it has failed the test of meaning, sensitivity, decency, and responsibility to the future.

6. Sexuality Has Value Only in a Permanent Relationship.

In the Jewish view, it is insufficient to affirm that the act must have meaning: it must also have value. For Judaism, value in human sexuality comes only when the relationship involves two people who have committed themselves to one another and have made that commitment in a binding covenant recognized by G-d and by society. The act of sexual union, the deepest personal statement that any human being can make, must be reserved for the moment of total oneness.

The sexual act is the first and most significant event of married life, and its force and beauty should not be compromised by sharing coitus in the expectation that some day a decision will be made to marry or not to marry. The act of sex is not only a declaration of present love, it is a covenantal statement of permanent commitment. It is only in this frame of reference that sexual congress is legitimate, because only then is it a religious act, a *de'var mitzvah*.

Love by itself is not a sufficient motivation for sexual expression; love that is authentic will want to reserve the ultimate act for the ultimate commitment. The test of a good marriage is not compatibility in bed, but compatibility in life. Given love and respect, sexual technique can be learned. Engaging in sex to "test it out" de-sanctifies the act. It is not a rehearsal for marriage, it is a rehearsal for divorce.

The Torah speaks of the sexual act as carnal knowledge, as in (Genesis 4:1) "Adam knew his wife Eve" (Gen. 4:1). *Ye'diah* is the most sublime human knowledge

because it knows the mystery, the soul of the beloved. In the sexual act, knowledge comes not only from physical intimacy and harmony and oneness, but also from experiencing the very depths of passion and extremes of emotion emanating from the loved one. It is knowledge from the inside. All such knowledge has two aspects: We learn about the other person, and we also experience ourselves at the extreme of our potential. Perhaps that is why taboos surround both love and death. A taboo is designed to protect us where we are most vulnerable and most mysterious—as we generate life in the privacy of our room, and as we take leave of life.

The increasing freedom from sexual restraint in this post-Freudian era is testimony to the demystification of sex and the irretrievable loss of precious "knowledge." We can conjecture further that perhaps the use of the term *yada* (revealing knowledge) for the sex act is contingent upon the prior existence of hiddenness, mystery. This *he-alem*, (concealment) exists both on the biological level—the internality of the female genitalia—and the societal—the idea of modesty, *tze'niut*, and its use of clothing to cover the body. As society sheds its clothing, there is progressively less to "know" by means of sexual exploration. If the object of carnal knowledge is to know our self as well as our mate, then the demystification of sex adversely affects our self-knowledge as well.

7. Sexuality Needs to Be Sanctified.

If sexuality is that deepest personal statement, filled with ecstasy and informed by knowledge, it follows that even within marriage sex is not considered simply a legitimated biological function. The Torah motivated the Jew to sanctify sex within marriage, for sex as a part of daily routine threatens to become wearisome and a dread bore, and sometimes more divisive than supportive. The laws of "family purity," which require abstinence during and shortly following the menstrual period, place the sexual act in a special category.

On a basic level, sanctity means separating oneself consciously from immorality and illicit thoughts. Maimonides incorporates the laws of sexual morality in a section of *Kedushah* (the Book of Holiness), and states that the deliberate separation from the illicit is an act of self-transcendence that constitutes sanctification. Ramban goes beyond Maimonides in his comment on the verse in Leviticus "Be you holy" (19:2): "Sanctify yourself even with that permitted you" is a call to those who strive to a higher level of spirituality and sensitivity to separate themselves from gross acts and uncouth behavior, even that which is technically permitted, so as not to become *naval bi-re'shut ha-Torah*, "a knave within the realm of the Torah."

Kiddushin—which signifies sanctity and betrothal—leads inevitably to *nissuin*—nuptials, elevation. Thus sanctification raises the physiological act of sex onto a higher, more spiritual level. This understanding of sanctity as leading to elevation is implied in the suggestion of the Talmud that it is preferable for a pious scholar to perform the conjugal act on the Sabbath. Rashi explains, "It is the night of joy, of rest, and of bodily pleasure." Such an affirmation is descriptive of how the Sabbath invested even bodily joys such as wearing special clothes and eating special foods with a special significance, elevating them to the realm of sanctified physical pleasures.

Sanctity also implies mystery. The Holy of Holies of the Temple, its inner sanctum, was visited only once every year, and then only by the High Priest. In the imagination of the people, it was a subject of awe and mystery.

Our society has lost the sense of the sacred, and there is little mystery attached to sex. Its physiology and technique have become commonplace to children, and teenagers are already tired and bored veterans.

Judaism teaches that the erotic act has wide significance, and that this physical act operates transcendentally. The creation of family and the consecration of marriage are events of which Jews sing at the wedding feast, *she-ha-simchah bi-me'ono*, "There is joy in His [G-d's] abode."

There are two terms for the sexual act. The better known is that which is used in the Bible and Talmud, *bi'ah*, which means "a coming" as in "he came unto her." The second is a Kabbalistic term, *chibbur*, which means "joining." It is used in *Iggeret ha-Kodesh*, which is subtitled *Sefer Chibbur Adam ve Ishto*, "The Book of Joining of Man and His Wife." The word and concept are based on the mystical vision of the cherubim facing and embracing one another in spiritual mutuality. It also connotes the ideal of *ye'diah*, "knowledge from the inside." The Kabbalah considers knowledge and joining synonymous—true "knowledge" derives only from an interpenetrating and joining of the two bodies, the knower and the to-be-known.

Where *bi'ah* is simply descriptive of the physical position of the male, *chibbur* implies a coming together of equals. While rape or seduction must be referred to as *bi'ah*, *chibbur* implies a need for consent.

Chibbur also recalls the fundamental Jewish mystical drive of uniting and mending into oneness the fragmented world of "broken vessels." Genesis records the separation of the rib from ancient Adam, and *chibbur* refers to the rejoining of that rib to the side of Adam. Judaism strives for an understanding and an affirmation of the concept of *chibbur* in the context of *yichud*, the mutual love of husband and wife. The contemporary writer I. Lewald says: "In the consciousness of belonging together, in the sense of constancy, resides the sanctity, the beauty of matrimony, which helps us to endure pain more easily, to enjoy happiness doubly, and to give rise to the fullest and finest development of our nature."

The Jewish Way in Love and Marriage [New York: Jonathan David Publishers, 1991], 24–34
Reprinted with permission of the publisher

Your Honeymoon Should Never End: How Separation Creates Fiery Love

by **Rabbi Manis Friedman**

There are two kinds of human love: the intrinsic, calm love that we feel for people to whom we're related by birth; and the more intimate, fiery love that exists in marriage. This is why the husband-wife relationship is very different from the parent-child relationship.

The love within a family, between relatives who are born of the same flesh, is innate. The love between a mother and child, a brother and sister, two brothers, two sisters, comes easily. Since they're related by nature, they feel comfortable with each other. There's an innate closeness between them, so their love is strong, solid, steady, predictable, and calm. There's no distance that has to be bridged; no difference that has to be overcome.

The love between a husband and wife isn't like that. Their love wasn't always there; they didn't always know each other; they weren't always related. No matter how well they get to know one another, they aren't alike. They are different from each other physically, emotionally, and mentally. They love each other in spite of the differences and because of them, but there isn't enough of a commonality between them to create a casual, calm love. The differences remain even after they are married, and the love between them will have to overcome these differences.

After all, husband and wife were once strangers. Male is different from female, so in essence they must remain strangers. Because of this, the love between them can never be casual, consistent, or calm.

This acquired love is naturally more intense than the love between brother and sister. When love has to overcome a difference, a distance, an obstacle, it needs energy to leap across and bridge the gap. This is the energy of fiery love.

Because the gap between husband and wife will never really close, their love for one another will continually have to reach across it. There will be distance, separation, then a bridging of distance, and a coming back together, again and again. This sense of distance intensifies the desire to merge.

To come together, man and woman have to overcome certain resistances. A man has to overcome his resistance to commitment, and a woman has to overcome her resistance to invasion. So, in coming together, husband and wife are reaching across great emotional distances, which intensifies their love. The absence of innate love actually makes the heart grow fonder.

If a brother and sister were to have a fiery love, their relationship would suffer. It's not the appropriate emotion for a brother and sister to have. Their love thrives when it's unbroken, unchallenged, constant, and calm. Not that they can't have disagreements, but those disagreements don't disrupt their love.

On the other hand, if a husband and wife develop a calm love for each other, their relationship will not thrive. If they are too familiar with each other, too comfortable with each other, like brother and sister, their love will not flourish. True intimacy in marriage—fiery love—is created by constant withdrawal and reunion.

If a husband and wife are never separate, their love begins to sour, because they are not creating an environment appropriate to that love. The environment of constant togetherness is not conducive to man-woman love; it's the environment for brother-sister love or parent-child love.

That's why the ideal blessing for a married couple is, "Your honeymoon should never end." A honeymoon—when two people who were once separate come together for the first time—should never end, because that's what a marriage thrives on.

The love between a man and a woman thrives on withdrawal and reunion, separation and coming together.

The only way to have an environment conducive to that kind of relationship is to provide a separation.

There are many kinds of separations. A couple can live in different places, have differences of opinion, or get into arguments and be angry at each other. Often the arguing isn't for the sake of arguing, but for the sake of creating a distance so that husband and wife can feel like they're coming together.

That's not a very happy solution. Making up after an argument may be good for a marriage on occasion, but not on a regular basis. It isn't a good idea to go looking for arguments, especially since separations can take a more positive form.

The physical separation given to us by G-d for that purpose is a much happier solution. That separation is created by observing a collection of laws described in Leviticus as "the laws of family purity," but more frequently referred to as the "laws of *mikvah*" (Lev. 15:19–33). The word *mikvah* refers to the ritual bath in which traditional Jewish women, since the days of the Bible, have immersed themselves following their monthly period and before renewing sexual relations with their husbands.

According to these laws of *mikvah*, during the time that a Jewish woman is menstruating, and for one week afterward, she is physically off-limits to her husband. For those days, the physical separation is total: no touching, no sitting on a swing together, and even sleeping in separate beds.

Through the ages, all sorts of explanations have been given for the laws described in Leviticus, but all of them have one thing in common: Separation protects and nurtures the intimate aspect of marriage, which thrives on withdrawal and reunion.

This understanding is not unique to Jews. In most cultures throughout the world, the ancients practiced varying degrees of separation between husband and wife during the woman's menstrual period. Some, such as certain tribes of American Indians, actually had separate living quarters, menstruant tents, where a woman would stay during her period. Later these customs deteriorated into myths, taboos, fears, superstitions, hygienic arguments, and other rationalizations, in an attempt to make sense of a delicate and sensitive subject.

But separation was such a universal practice that I wonder if human beings know instinctively that male-female love thrives on withdrawal and reunion, on coming together following a separation. The body is actually reflecting an emotional state. Just as the love between man and woman cannot be maintained at full intensity all the time, but needs a certain creative tension without which it will not flourish, the body has a similar need.

As far as Jews are concerned, we know these cyclical changes were created for that very purpose. This is much more than a coincidence: It is how the body reflects the soul, how the body is created in the image of the soul.

Like everything else that exists in our lives, the cycle of withdrawal and reunion that exists in marriage is meant to be a reflection of our relationship with G-d. The two kinds of love, calm love and fiery love, exist not only among human beings, but between ourselves and G-d.

When we refer to G-d as our Father, it's an innate and intrinsic relationship. We don't have to work for it; it's just there. It's a steady, constant love, an indestructible love, a love compared to water—calm love.

But we also talk about how G-d is infinite and we are finite; G-d is true and we are not; G-d is everything and we are barely something. Because of these differences, we feel a great distance from G-d, and the need to create a relationship with Him. Establishing a relationship in spite of the differences, in spite of the distance, is more like a marriage. That's a stormy relationship—fiery love.

More precisely, our soul loves G-d like a child loves a parent, because our soul is of G-d. That love is innate and calm. When G-d tells this soul to go down into a body, that's a separation. Then our soul loves G-d with a fiery love, which, like the love between a husband and wife, does not come automatically. Acquired love is by nature intense and fiery.

Eventually, the soul will be reunited with G-d more intimately than before, just as the intimacy between a husband and wife is deeper when they come together following a separation. Therefore, when G-d says that a husband and wife have to be modest with one another, that they may be together and then separate, come together and separate again, according to a monthly cycle, it's not an artificial imposition. It may produce discipline, which is nice. It may keep the marriage fresh, which is important. But there's more to it than that.

It is, in fact, the natural reflection of the type of love that must exist between husband and wife. In order to nurture that stormy, fiery love, our way of living has to correspond to the emotions we are trying to nurture and retain.

If there's going to be a separation—and there needs to be one—consider the following: Rather than wait for a separation to develop, where a husband and wife get into a fight or lose interest in each other, let's take the cue from the body and create a physical, rather than emotional, separation.

Everyone is saying, "I need my space." It's true. Keeping the laws of *mikvah,* when they apply, is one way of creating that space; other laws of modesty might be beneficial as well. For example, husband and wife need not touch each other casually or in public; they should avoid casual nudity; and vulgarities, which are inappropriate in mixed company, should also be inappropriate for the home.

In giving us these laws, G-d tells us: "The marriage love, unlike the family love, unlike the born love, thrives when you separate and come back together. But rather than create an internal, emotional separation, create an external separation by keeping the laws of modesty. Don't separate emotionally; separate physically, and come back together emotionally."

Since the love between husband and wife is one of reaching across distances, of the constant bridging of

a gulf, and only that kind of intimate, fiery love is appropriate for husband and wife, our physical behavior has to reflect and support that emotional state. We do that by being modest.

Doesn't Anyone Blush Anymore?: Reclaiming Intimacy, Modesty, and Sexuality [San Francisco: Harper San Franscisco, 1990], 71–76
Reprinted with permission of the author

Intimacy: The Sanctity of Sexuality

by **Rabbi Simon Jacobson**

The dignity of the princess is *within, more than the golden clothing which she wears.*
—Psalms 45:14

If you are close when you should be distant, you will be distant when you should be close.
—The Rebbe

The Rebbe, in a conversation with a psychologist, once expressed the great need in society for an awareness of the proper guidelines and boundaries of intimacy. This was necessary, he said, in order to establish and preserve healthy marriages, which are the bedrock of a sound society. In 1975, the Rebbe called upon the worldwide chapters of the Lubavitch Women's Organization to establish committees to publish literature and classes dealing with intimacy.

What Are Sexuality and Intimacy?

In regard to intimacy, we live in a time of crisis. Everyone craves intimacy, and everyone is searching for intimacy, yet it has become an area of great conflict and confusion.

There are many forces at work. Society's standards of sexuality and intimacy have changed greatly since the so-called sexual revolution. Ours is now a society bombarded by sexual thought and imagery; sexual boundaries have been blurred.

It is obviously an appropriate time to review our attitude toward intimacy and sexuality. What is sexuality exactly, and what is the power behind its mystique? What deeper meaning does it have in our lives? Are intimacy and sexuality one and the same? The "sexual revolution" supposedly set people free; are *you* free, or are you enslaved more than ever to your desires, more confused than ever by shifting standards?

Sexuality is an internal, G-dly energy, a meeting of body and soul, that is nourished by true intimacy, by modesty and subtlety. It can only flourish in a healthy manner in the context of the sacred institution of marriage. Sexuality itself possesses both a body and a soul, a physical and spiritual dimension. Its body is the union of human bodies, accompanied by the deepest of physical pleasures. Its soul is the union with G-dliness, accompanied by the deepest of spiritual pleasures. When sexuality's spiritual nature is removed or ignored, it can become an irrational obsession that consumes an individual.

Sexuality is among the most potent forces in life. It can either lift us to the greatest heights of self-sacrifice and commitment or lower us into the depths of self-interest and demoralization. Sexuality is never neutral.

The irony is that focusing on sexuality is its undoing. Sexuality divorced of its intimate nature loses its true meaning, its dignity, its majesty. This is where sexuality and intimacy diverge. Intimacy does not equal sexuality; it is a special state, separate from all else in our lives, that must be approached with gentleness and awe. In the Bible, sexuality is called "knowledge," for it involves intimate knowledge shared by two people. When sexuality loses its intimacy and is seen in the same light as our other bodily needs, it becomes base hedonism, little more than a technical and biological function.

Because human beings tend to define things in physical terms, using only our sensory tools instead of our spiritual tools, we often ignore sexuality's spiritual component. Its powerful hold on man becomes a purely physical hold, defined individually by each person. Only by understanding the soul of sexuality, which is healthy intimacy, can we uncover the root of its power and passion.

A young woman came to see a rabbi, saying she was having difficulty finding an appropriate spouse. The rabbi suggested that she concentrate on communicating verbally with her prospective mates, in order to see if they were truly compatible, and to avoid any intimacy. "But in today's society," the woman responded, "that is simply unrealistic."

The rabbi sighed and said quietly, "Intimacy is like fire. When you think you will quench it by indulging it, you quickly realize that you are pouring gasoline, not water, on the fire. However, when intimacy is experienced with discipline, within the context of a sanctified marriage, it becomes a fire that warms both people and illuminates their home and family."

Why Is Sexuality So Powerful?

When G-d created man and woman, they were one human in the image of one G-d; then they were separated into two distinct parts. "Therefore," as is written in Genesis, "a man shall leave his father and his mother and be united with his wife, and they shall become one flesh."

Man and woman constantly feel this need to reunite. And sexuality is this union. Man and woman seek to "become one flesh," thereby uniting with G-d, in whose image they were created. No wonder intimacy is such a powerful force: It is the only experience in human life in which we come face to face with G-d.

Intimacy is also the only experience in life that allows us to become truly G-dlike, in that it empowers a husband and wife to create. Nothing else we do as human beings is as G-dlike as creating a new life, which in turn can create other lives, on and on, into eternity. This G-dly nature is what gives sexuality its mystique; it is the one opportunity man has to "taste" G-d—to think as He thinks, to create as He creates.

In addition, intimacy is a celebration of vulnerability; it touches the softest spot in each person, the most private and fragile part of a human being. Therefore, we must cultivate a healthy environment for our intimacy, one that allows us to appreciate and revel in this vulnerability, secure and protected.

Most of us desire true intimacy, but we are afraid to experience true vulnerability, to lose control. But this makes it difficult to ever experience true intimacy, for being comfortable with your vulnerability is the ultimate intimacy. The *illusion* of intimacy—where each person is getting what he or she needs—only makes people feel good at the moment, if at all. If they are still in control at the end, if they have not exposed their vulnerability, then their "intimacy" was just another form of exercising control over another person.

The question is, How can we really let go? Maybe we simply can't. Human beings are weak, we say; we simply don't have the ability to truly trust one another. That might be the case if we were animals, but we are not—we are G-dly, our souls infused with the spirit of G-d, who gave us the capacity to love as He does. When we learn to see the G-dliness in each other, we can begin to trust, and reach beyond our own self-contained distrusting selves and to experience real love and intimacy. We, then, can choose to let go and be vulnerable, to be ourselves without putting up our defenses, without fear of abuse.

As with all matters, we have been given a choice. We can be distracted and misled by the physical passion of intimacy, pursuing it only to satisfy our selfish needs, which then drives man and woman apart. Or we can understand sexuality and intimacy as the truly meaningful forces that they are, as the means to connect with G-d in the most powerful, sublime manner, which in turn unites man and woman as one.

How Do We Experience Healthy Intimacy?

Healthy intimacy requires two ingredients: discipline and sanctification. We must exercise self-control, and we must also see sexuality as sacred.

One must approach the sanctity of sexuality with awe, like entering into the Holy of Holies, where every action counts, where any blemish is intolerable. We must experience sexuality in a controlled environment with appropriate boundaries—not to dampen the expression of love, but to channel the powerful physical energies into healthy passion.

In modern society, sexuality often involves two people who are each interested only in satisfying their own needs. But sexuality is meant to be *transcendent,* not indulgent, allowing you to let another person inside your soul so you can build something greater together. Only by introducing G-d into the relationship can a man and woman overcome their individual desires, and marriage is the only perfect environment in which to do so. In all other environments, intimacy is unhealthy and harmful.

And yet, how often are we victims of our own sexuality, allowing our unchecked needs and desires to control our decisions? How often do we use sexuality to distract ourselves from existential pain, mistakenly believing we can remedy a deep-seated problem with a superficial solution?

The key to healthy intimacy is to stop the vicious cycle of untamed sexuality, for the more you feed it the hungrier it gets. Discipline and subtlety direct these into a healthy and growthful experience.

The argument that one must first try living with another person before deciding whether to marry is not valid. When sexuality is experienced in an inappropriate manner, it only hampers our ability to achieve true intimacy when the time is right; if you are close when you should be distant, you will be distant when you should be close. But when intimacy is experienced properly, we achieve closeness that flows into the rest of our lives and introduces sanctity and unity into all that we do. Intimacy is an integral part of our lives and cannot be compartmentalized. It is part of building a home and family, a full and complete life.

Healthy intimacy must also be modest. By definition, intimacy is quiet and discreet. Upon their creation, man and woman "were both naked but they were not ashamed." They were as innocent as children, seeing sexuality only as a part of G-d's creation and designed to serve a sacred function. But after they transgressed and ate from the Tree of Knowledge, they lost their innocence: "The eyes of both of them were opened, and they realized that they were naked." They experienced a healthy shame stemming from modesty, and they covered themselves.

The only members of our society today who are not self-conscious about their sexuality are children, for they are born with an innate sense of modesty. This modesty needs to be cultivated and nurtured by parents and educators. Ideally, we would all be as innocent as children. Sexuality would flow from a healthy spirit and soul. We would learn about healthy intimacy simply by being around our healthy parents and grandparents.

But in these turbulent times, such lessons are not so easily gained, and this concept of modesty must be articulated. Young people today are more than willing to be taught an alternative to our current standards, but they are caught in a whirlwind of peer pressure. It is the responsibility of teachers, parents, and every sort of leader to teach them about the sanctity of sexuality.

So we must strive to realize that true intimacy, the authentic dignity of a human being, shines from within. What kind of message is being sent by someone who dresses provocatively or who speaks of sexuality without the proper respect? Such overt sexuality only promotes sexist attitudes that further distort how we look at our fellow human beings. True beauty, one that commands both love and respect, is inner beauty.

It is true, especially in contemporary society, that people don't want anyone to impose restrictions on their sexuality. But not all forms of sexual behavior are acceptable. The sanctity of sexuality obviously requires behavior that follows the divine laws of our creator, laws that do not ask us to deny sexuality but to experience it in healthy and intimate forms that will enhance human growth and progress, and break the chains of enslavement to one's passions that ultimately leads to societal decadence.

The fact that we live in a society that is largely unfamiliar with healthy sexuality does not change this truth. And even if a particular aberrant sexual desire were thought to be genetic, for instance, it should still not be condoned, for much of our very existence is concerned with properly channeling our natural desires.

Still, we must distinguish between a person and a person's *behavior*. Establishing a standard of behavior should not be used to invalidate one who does not live by it; these standards—which are uncompromisable—are meant to give us clarity and the ability to improve our behavior. G-d's standard for human sexuality is what is best for each of us, and we must not be afraid to teach these ideals. As with communicating all serious matters of truth, we must do so sensitively, speaking with genuine love and concern but also with discipline, in a manner and language that emphasize the positive and motivate one to grow.

The current crisis surrounding sexuality in our society must be seen as an opportunity to explore its importance. During recent years, we have clearly witnessed that immodest sexual behavior does nothing to cultivate true intimacy. It only destroys the respect for the individual and for home and family. But we have also begun to see a growing consciousness that puts more emphasis on communication, both intellectually and emotionally, than on promiscuous sexual behavior, and that is clearly a step in the right direction.

The time has come to reclaim our sexuality and intimacy, to return them to the context of marriage, home, and family. The time has come to reintroduce G-d into our intimate lives, to populate and civilize the world, to "become one flesh," and to return to our original intimacy with our creator. This would be a true sexual revolution. Take this responsibility seriously. An entire world—beginning with your own small world—hangs in the balance.

The Rebbe was once asked his opinion concerning sex education in the schools. "Discussing such an issue does help resolve a problem," the Rebbe answered, "but as the sages tell us, the more you discuss sexuality, the more you instigate. Therefore, great care must be taken in this area. It should be done by sensitive professionals who will avoid any provocative expressions or associations. It should be discussed privately with a student, or at most with two or three students, and it should be discussed separately with boys and girls, to keep the boundaries clear."

Toward a Meaningful Life: The Wisdom of the Rebbe [New York, NY: William Morrow, 1995], 66–73
Reprinted with permission of www.meaningfullife.com

Lesson 3

Will My Spouse Ever Change?
What You Can Do About Character Flaws

Introduction

Is the process of improving a marriage a joint venture, or is it an individual one? Is it one in which two individuals embark upon simultaneous parallel journeys, or is it a single journey with two passengers?

The Solo Tango
Unilateral Marriage?

Learning Interaction 1

Imagine you encountered a genie. "Hey," the genie says, "I'm in a generous mood, and I heard that you joined *The Art of Marriage* course. That tells me that you are looking to upgrade your relationship with your spouse. What is the one factor or relationship dynamic that, if changed, will bring the greatest enhancement to your marriage? Tell me what that is and I'll change it for you."

What would be your response?

To be accepted for who you are.

Find the "Pro-Found" Difference

Text **1a**

מָצָא אִשָּׁה מָצָא טוֹב, וַיָּפֶק רָצוֹן מֵה׳.

משלי יח,כב

e who has found a woman has found goodness, and he will elicit God's favor.

Proverbs 18:22

Text **1b**

וּמוֹצֶא אֲנִי מַר מִמָּוֶת אֶת הָאִשָּׁה.

קהלת ז,כו

 find bitterer than death the woman.

Ecclesiastes 7:26

Text 1c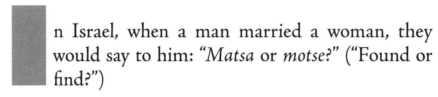

```
"?מצא או מוצא" :במערבא, כי נסיב איניש אתתא, אמרי ליה הכי
."'מצא—דכתיב, "מצא אשה מצא טוב ויפק רצון מה
."מוצא—דכתיב: "ומוצא אני מר ממות את האשה
תלמוד בבלי, ברכות ח,א
```

Babylonian Talmud. A literary work of monumental proportions that draws upon the totality of the legal, spiritual, intellectual, ethical, and historical traditions of Judaism, the Babylonian Talmud was set up as a commentary to the Mishnah and was written primarily in Aramaic. The Talmud contains the teachings of the Jewish sages, mostly from the period after the destruction of the Second Temple through the fifth century C.E. The Babylonian Talmud has served as the primary vehicle for the education of countless Jews over the centuries; it is the entry point for all subsequent legal, ethical, and theological Jewish scholarship.

n Israel, when a man married a woman, they would say to him: *"Matsa* or *motse?"* ("Found or find?")

"Matsa," as it is written: "He who has found (*matsa*) a woman has found goodness."

"Motse," as it is written: "I find (*motse*) bitterer than death the woman."

Talmud, Berachot 8a

Text 2

n the first verse the verb ("he who has found") is followed directly by its object ("a woman"), implying that what the husband has sought and found is indeed his wife. His mind and heart focus on her, and his conscious concern is to meet her needs and the needs of his family, as opposed to his own. This is the foundation of a happy married life.

In the second verse, however (which, in the original, literally reads: "and find I bitterer than death the woman"), the subject ("I") is interposed *between* the verb ("find") and its object ("woman")—as if the subject of the verb were also its primary object—thereby implying that the man is really more concerned with finding himself—i.e., with his own self-gratification.

Rabbi Yitzchak Ginsburgh, *The Mystery of Marriage* [Jerusalem: Gal Einai, 1999], p. 3

Rabbi Yitzchak Ginsburgh (1944–). A renowned teacher and author on Jewish mysticism, born in S. Louis, Missouri, and immigrated to Israel in 1965. He has authored many works in both Hebrew and English and lectures internationally, endeavoring to make the teachings of Kabbalah spiritually relevant to the modern person.

Optional Section

Question for Discussion

Why are these proverbs, which present seemingly gender-neutral marriage advice, presented from the male standpoint?

Text 3a

Men and women live within contexts of independence or interdependence, respectively. Consequently, their goals, activities, plans, interactions, values, and self-systems are continually shaped by these contexts. . . .

Although there is certainly great variation within the genders in the degree to which self-construals reflect gender stereotypes and gendered social roles, we assume that women are more likely than men to develop an interdependent self-construal, whereas men are more likely than women to develop an independent self-construal.

Susan E. Cross and Laura Madson, "Models of the Self: Self-Construals and Gender," *Psychological Bulletin*, 1997, Vol. 122, No. 1, 5–37

Susan E. Cross. Professor in the department of psychology at Iowa State University, her research focuses on how people define themselves and on exploring the consequences of self-definition for thinking, feeling, and behaving.

Laura Madson. Associate professor of psychology at New Mexico State University, her primary interests are gender, sexuality, and the scholarship of teaching.

Text 3b

Although individuals with an independent self-construal certainly desire relationships, their relationships often reflect individualistic goals. Relationships with others may serve as mirrors for the individual's comparison of the self with others, as backdrops for the self-enhancing display of abilities or attributes, or as a means to demonstrate uniqueness by an assertion of dominance over others. For these persons, individual rights, goals, and wishes are the primary basis for moral choices. The goals and needs of society, family members, or others are secondary or subordinate to the individual's. . . .

For the person with an interdependent self-construal, relationships are viewed as integral parts of the person's very being. Indeed, one's thoughts, feelings, and wishes may be interpreted and understood in light of the thoughts, feelings, and behaviors of close others, in contrast to the wariness of another's influence which is characteristic of the independent self-construal. For individuals with an interdependent self-construal, obligations to others and responsiveness to the needs of others shape moral decisions and social interactions. The goals and needs of family and close others are often as important as one's own goals and needs.

Susan E. Cross and Laura Madson, ibid.

End of Optional Section

His and Hers Advice

Learning Interaction 2

Rate the importance of the following three emotions, assigning each a number from 1 to 3 (1 means most important, 3 means least important).

	Love	Respect	Reverence
Husband towards wife	*1*	*2*	*3*
Wife towards husband	*1*	*2*	*3*

Text 4

צוו חכמים שיהא אדם מכבד את אשתו יותר מגופו, ואוהבה כגופו. ואם יש לו ממון, מרבה בטובתה כפי ממונו. ולא יטיל עליה אימה יתירה, ויהיה דבורו עמה בנחת ולא יהיה עצב ולא רגזן.

וכן צוו על האשה שתהיה מכבדת את בעלה ביותר מדאי, ויהיה עליה מורא ממנו ותעשה כל מעשיה על פיו. ויהיה בעיניה כמו שר או מלך, מהלכת בתאות לבו ומרחקת כל מה שישנא.

וזה דרך בנות ישראל ובני ישראל הקדושים והטהורים בזיווגן, ובדרכים אלו יהיה ישובן נאה ומשובח.

משנה תורה, הלכות אישות טו,יט–כ

Rabbi Moshe ben Maimon
(1135–1204). Better known
as Maimonides or by the
acronym Rambam; born in
Cordoba, Spain. After the
conquest of Cordoba by the
Almohads, he fled Spain and
eventually settled in Cairo,
Egypt. There, he became the
leader of the Jewish community and served as court physician to the vizier of Egypt. His
rulings on Jewish law are considered integral to the formation of halachic consensus.
He is most noted for authoring the *Mishneh Torah,* an
encyclopedic arrangement of
Jewish law, and for his philosophical work, *Guide for the
Perplexed.*

ur sages instructed that a man honor his wife more than he honors himself and love her as he loves himself. If he has riches, he should use it to benefit her in accordance with his means. He should never impose excessive fear upon [his wife]; he should talk with her gently; and he should exhibit neither sadness nor anger.

Our sages instructed that a woman honor her husband exceedingly and accord him reverence. She should carry out all her deeds according to his directives and consider him like a minister or king. She should follow the desires of his heart and shun all things that he despises.

This is the manner of holy and pure Jewish women and men in their marriages. [By following] these ways the marriage will be pleasant and praiseworthy.

Maimonides, *Mishneh Torah*, Laws of Marriage 15:19–20

Figure **3.1**

	Respect	**Love**	**Reverence**	**Not to Get Angry**
Husband towards wife	✓	✓	x	✓
Wife towards husband	✓	x	✓	x

Why Love Isn't Enough
Fishy Love

Questions for Discussion

1. What is the difference between love and respect?
2. Can one respect but not love, or vice versa?
3. Which of the two is more important in a relationship?

Text 5

There is a Jewish folktale that illustrates how vague the meaning of the word "love" can be, and also demonstrates some of the basic problems in statements such as "I love you."

Once upon a time, a fisherman caught a large pike, and when he pulled the fish out of the water and saw its size, he said, "This is wonderful! I'll take it to the Baron; he loves pike." The poor fish says to himself, "There's some hope for me yet."

The fisherman brings the fish to the manor house, and the guard says, "What do you have?"

"A pike."

"Great," says the guard. "The Baron loves pike."

The fish feels that there is some corroboration of the facts.

Rabbi Adin Steinsaltz (Even-Yisrael) (1937–). Born in Jerusalem, Steinsaltz is considered one of the foremost Jewish thinkers of the 20th century. Praised by *Time* as a "once-in-a-millennium scholar," he has been awarded the Israel Prize for his contributions to Jewish study. He is the founder of the Israel Institute for Talmudic Publications, a society dedicated to the translation and elucidation of the Talmud.

The fisherman enters the palace, and though the fish can hardly breathe, he still has hope: the Baron loves pike. He is brought into the kitchen, and all the cooks exclaim how much the Baron loves pike. The fish is placed on a table, and the Baron himself enters and gives instructions, "Cut off the tail, cut off the head, and slit it this way."

With his last breath, the fish cries out in great despair, "Why did you lie? You don't love pike, you love yourself!"

Rabbi Adin Steinsaltz, *Simple Words* [New York: Simon & Schuster, 1999], pp. 190–191

Due Respect

Text 6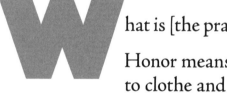

איזהו כיבוד? . . . כיבוד: מאכיל ומשקה, מלביש ומכסה, מכניס ומוציא.
תלמוד בבלי, קידושין לא,ב

What is [the practical definition of] honor?

Honor means to feed and provide drink, to clothe and cover, to lead in and out.

Talmud, Kidushin 31b

Gender Differences
Beyond Chivalry

Text 7

When men and women take personality tests, some of the old Mars-Venus stereotypes keep reappearing. On average, women are more cooperative, nurturing, cautious and emotionally responsive. Men tend to be more competitive, assertive, reckless and emotionally flat. Clear differences appear in early childhood and never disappear.

What's not clear is the origin of these differences. Evolutionary psychologists contend that these are innate traits inherited from ancient hunters and gatherers. Another school of psychologists asserts that both sexes' personalities have been shaped by traditional social roles, and that personality differences will shrink as women spend less time nurturing children and more time in jobs outside the home.

To test these hypotheses, a series of research teams have repeatedly analyzed personality tests taken by men and women in more than 60 countries around the world. For evolutionary psychologists, the bad news is that the size of the gender gap in personality varies among cultures. For social-role psychologists, the bad news is that the variation is going in the wrong direction. It looks as if personality differences between men and women are smaller in traditional cultures like India's or Zimbabwe's than in the Netherlands or the United

John Tierney. Author and journalist, he has been with *The New York Times* since 1990 and has written extensively about science, technology, economics, and environmental controversies.

States. A husband and a stay-at-home wife in a patriarchal Botswanan clan seem to be more alike than a working couple in Denmark or France. The more Venus and Mars have equal rights and similar jobs, the more their personalities seem to diverge.

John Tierney, "As Barriers Disappear, Some Gender Gaps Widen," *The New York Times*, September 8, 2008

Text 8

לעולם יהא אדם זהיר בכבוד אשתו.

תלמוד בבלי, בבא מציעא נט,א

A man should always be especially scrupulous to accord his wife honor.

Talmud, Bava Metsi'a 59a

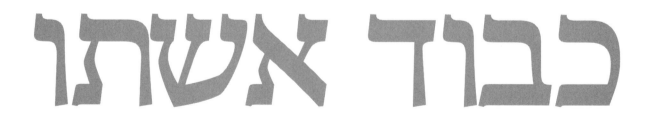

כבוד אשתו

Research on social support and marriage has repeatedly found that emotional support from a spouse is a significant predictor of both greater marital satisfaction and less marital conflict—and more so for women than for men. Emotional support is thought to be more important for women's well-being.

Kristin D. Mickelson et al., "The Moderating Role of Gender and Gender Role Attitudes on the Link Between Spousal Support and Marital Quality," *Sex Roles* 55, no. 1–2 (2006), p. 74

EMOTIONAL SUPPORT

Who Is the Boss?

Text 10

אין לך אשה כשרה בנשים אלא אשה שהיא עושה רצון בעלה.

תנא דבי אליהו רבה, ט

An upright woman is one who actualizes her husband's wishes.

Tana Devei Eliyahu Rabah 9

Learning Interaction 3

The following two lists are from *How to Improve Your Marriage Without Talking About It* by Patricia Love and Steven Stosny.[1] The first is a list of how a woman can "shame a man without trying." The second is a list of things a man can do to fill the "void that exists in a woman's life."

Can you discern the difference between the marital advice dispensed to the man and to the woman?

---

[1] New York: Broadway Books, 2007, pp. 67–69, 81–82.

How a woman can "shame a man without trying"

Excluding him from important decisions

Robbing him of the opportunity to help

Correcting what he said

Questioning his judgment

Giving unsolicited advice

Ignoring his advice

Implying inadequacy

Making unrealistic demands of his time and energy

Overreacting (which is a form of criticizing his choices or behavior)

Ignoring his needs (basically sending the message that they're not important)

Focusing on what I didn't get, not what I did

Withholding praise

Using a harsh tone

Valuing others' needs over his

Undermining his wishes

Condescending

Name-calling

Belittling his work

Showing little or no interest in his interests

Criticizing his family

- Ignoring him
- Interpreting him
- Comparing
- Dismissing
- Focusing on my own unhappiness
- Expecting him to make me happy
- Making "you" statements
- Globalizing
- Generalizing
- "Therapizing"
- Projecting my unhappiness on him
- Believing [I] always know what's best for the relationship
- Rolling eyes
- Giving "the look"
- Being sarcastic
- Ridiculing
- Suggesting a "better way"
- Having unrealistic expectations
- Criticizing him in front of other people
- Making him feel unnecessary

Things a man can do to fill the "void that exists in a woman's life"

- Acknowledge that it is your responsibility, as well as hers, to keep your home life functioning satisfactorily.
- Appreciate all that she does for the home and family.
- Do your share of household chores, management, and meal preparation—make it less of a division of labor and more of a together activity.
- Do the chores you agreed to in a timely fashion.
- Notice what needs to be done and do it without being told, asked, or reminded.
- Willingly pay for help maintaining the residence.
- Notice when she makes home improvements.
- Pick up after yourself, and pick up after others.
- If you know her dreams, keep them in mind when you make decisions.
- If you don't know her dreams, pay attention and let her teach you.
- Understand that her dreams change —you need to continually update your information.
- Understand that her dreams are not the same as yours.

- Understand you have the ability to make her extremely happy.
- Understand you have the ability to make her extremely unhappy.
- Become the guardian of her dreams, and make fulfilling and honoring them a priority.
- Take pleasure in fulfilling and honoring her dreams.
- Suggest and plan activities that include her.
- Make sure that each week includes activities you enjoy together.
- Pay attention to her when you are out in public together.
- Develop rituals for time at home that include her, for example, drinking coffee together in the morning, cooking dinner together, watching birds together.
- Increase contact time with her—affectionate touching or shared activities when work hours get long.

Who Is the REAL Boss?

Text 11a

אמר לו הקדוש ברוך הוא למשה: "לך אמור לבנות ישראל אם רוצות לקבל את התורה, שדרכם של אנשים הולכים אחר דעתן של נשים".

פרקי רבי אליעזר מא

God said to Moses: "Go inquire of the Israelite women whether they wish to receive the Torah; for it is the nature of the men to follow the opinion of the women."

Pirkei Rabbi Eliezer 41

Pirkei Rabbi Eliezer ("Chapters of Rabbi Eliezer") is an early rabbinic work bearing the name of Rabbi Eliezer ben Hyrcanus, a prominent 1st–2nd-century sage. This *midrash* provides textual exegeses and stories, expounds upon the biblical narrative, and develops and illustrates moral principles. It commences with the story of the early days of Rabbi Eliezer's life and then proceeds to expound upon some major biblical themes, from Creation until the journey of the Israelites in the wilderness.

Question for Discussion

How can we reconcile this text, which asserts that it is the nature of men to follow the opinion of women, with Text 10, which maintains that an upright woman actualizes her husband's wishes?

Text 11b

"איזה אשה כשירה כל שהיא עושה רצון בעלה", דהיינו שהיא מולדת רצון בבעלה.

עבודת ישראל, פסח

"An upright woman is one who actualizes her husband's desire"—that is, she brings about her husband's desire.

Rabbi Yisrael Hopstein, *Avodat Yisrael*, Passover

Rabbi Yisrael Hopstein (ca. 1736–1815), a Chasidic rebbe known as the Magid (preacher) of Koznitz. He was a disciple of Rabbi Dov Ber of Mezritch and Rabbi Elimelech of Lizhensk. Among his many works is *Avodat Yisrael* (on the Bible) in which he displays mastery in both the legal and kabbalistic teachings of Judaism. Rabbi Yitschak Meir Alter, the founder of the dynasty of Ger, was one of his disciples.

The Missing Love and Anger

Text 12

Dr. Patricia Love. Widely published relationships educator and licensed marriage and family therapist, she is faculty emeritus at the Imago Institute for Relationship Therapy and a recipient of the Smart Marriages Impact Award. She is the author of *Hot Monogamy*, *The Truth About Love*, and co-authored *How to Improve Your Marriage Without Talking About It* with Steven Stosny.

Dr. Steven Stosny. Founder of CompassionPower, an organization dedicated to treating domestic violence and child abuse offenders, he has taught at the University of Maryland and at S. Mary's College of Maryland. His most recent books are *How to Improve Your Marriage Without Talking About It,* co-authored with Patricia Love, and *Love Without Hurt*.

Perhaps the most stressful form of isolation for a woman occurs when the person she would normally turn to for comfort is the source of threat. Men are frightening to women because of their brute strength and the heart-stopping force of their anger. Most men have no idea how frightening, threatening, and terrorizing their anger is to women. Even when the anger is not directed at the woman, it still has a frightening effect. An angry voice can trigger her fear response and dump cortisol into her system. If he has a habit of overreacting and getting angry on a regular basis, she lives in a constant state of fear and alertness. In addition, she cannot feel completely safe or relaxed with him—a prerequisite for love, affection, and *connection*.

Patricia Love and Steven Stosny, *How to Improve Your Marriage Without Talking About It* [New York: Broadway Books, 2007], pp. 79–80

Text 13

Where respect builds, anger destroys. Where true respect prevails, anger is not likely to come into play, for it is not usual to explode at people one really respects. The presence of anger thus points to a double deficit, in that the proper respect that should obtain in the marriage is sorely lacking.

Rabbi Reuven P. Bulka, *Jewish Marriage: A Halakhic Ethic* [Hoboken N.J.: Ktav Publishing Co., 1986], p. 50

Rabbi Dr. Reuven P. Bulka
(1944–). Rabbi, radio host, and columnist, he has served as rabbi of Congregation Machzikei Hadas in Ottawa, Ontario, since 1967. He received his PhD from the University of Ottawa in 1971, concentrating on Viktor Frankl's ideas about logotherapy. He is the founder and editor of the *Journal of Psychology and Judaism* and was co-president of the Canadian Jewish Congress from 2007–2009.

RESPECT

ANGER

Key Points

1. Love is not enough to sustain a relationship because it is rooted in self-love, a desire to satisfy one's own needs and desires. Respect, however, is the result of valuing the other for who he or she is. Thus, respect lies at the core of marriage.

2. Powerful love that is not tempered by respect can become overbearing and stifling. Respect for our spouses allows them space to make their own decisions, even if we don't agree with them.

3. The practical way to honor another person is to provide for his or her needs and ensure that he or she is cared for.

4. A woman's primary emotional need is to know that her husband respects her and her needs, and to feel that she is her husband's first priority. To provide this, he must put her needs and dignity before his own.

5. A man's primary needs in a relationship are to feel trusted, capable, and competent, and that he is "the man of the house."

6. A wise woman shapes the correct desires of her husband in a gentle way, without forcing him to relinquish his authority.

7. By identifying one's spouse's needs and making an effort to provide for them, one can increase the spark of love in the relationship and likely cause one's spouse to reciprocate.

Take-Home Exercise

It is a challenging yet very worthwhile exercise for spouses to clearly articulate their partner's mental, emotional, and physical needs.

Fill out the following chart at home. List, in order of importance, your own five greatest needs and what you feel are your partner's five greatest needs. Then describe how you wish to have your own needs fulfilled, and how you think you can fulfill your partner's deepest needs. (For example, you need respect; you want your spouse to supply that by giving you his/her undivided attention when you walk into the house after work.) Ask your spouse to fill out this chart too on a separate sheet of paper.

My Partner's Needs	How I Supply My Partner's Needs	My Needs	How I'd Like My Partner to Supply My Needs
1.		1.	
2.		2.	
3.		3.	
4.		4.	
5.		5.	

Then compare your chart with your spouse's. It should be an enlightening experience. You might discover that (1) your partner's needs are very different from what you thought they were; (2) even if you listed some or all of your partner's needs, your prioritization of the needs is askew; and (3) what you were doing to supply those needs is not how your partner wants/needs them supplied.

Additional Readings

Habits of Highly Successful Lovers: Secrets from the Kabbalah

by **Rabbi David Aaron**

What is life about? The Kabbalah teaches that the essence of life—the very theme of life—is love. What is the motivating drive in the world? What is driving us all, pushing us through? It is love. Ultimately, all people want to love and be loved. The funny thing is some of those popular songs are right—"Without love I am nothing, nothing at all" is actually true. And "All you need is love, love, love" is also true. But it's not so easy. It's a lot of work. Just how the Torah and Kabbalah teach us to do this is what we will examine in this article. To start off we need to understand how you and I came to be——the very dynamics of our creation.

The Kabbalah teaches that in the beginning, all of existence was the simple light of the Endless One (G-d). When the Endless One wanted to create the world, the Endless One caused the withdrawal of the light from the center, creating a spherical vacuum, creating space. Within this space, the Endless One created vessels. Unlike the Endless One, who was infinite, the vessels were finite. And while the vessels were created by and of the Endless One, they were also different from the Endless One. They were other and multiple. And being vessels or containers they were designed to receive, in contrast to the light, which gives. Then the Endless One projected a thin ray of endless light into the vessels. But each vessel was unable to independently receive the light, and so they broke. And existence went into the state of chaos. The Kabbalists tell us that life, the world and ourselves are the broken vessels, and that what we are trying to do is to mend ourselves and the world so that someday we may be able to receive the light without

breaking. The Kabbalists call this notion tikkun——meaning mending or fixing. Of course, I have given you this very deep mystical story in a very small nutshell. The Kabbalistic story is essentially the story of love. Life is the love story. Consider the parallel in your life, in the modern world, today. In the beginning, there is just you. In order to love, you need to withdraw yourself from the center and create a space for another. Love starts only when you do that—move yourself out of the way to make room for another person in your life. In other words, if you are self-centered you are not ready for love. If you are self-centered, you can't make enough space to nurture another. And true love is not only creating that space within your life for another, but also giving him or her that space and respecting and maintaining that space. It is being a part of another life and removed from that life at the same time.

Everybody needs his or her space. If you ever had the experience of having someone speak too close to your face, you know what it feels like to have your space invaded. I had a friend once who would do that. And by the end of the conversation I would find myself pinned against the wall, because all along I had been inadvertently backing away from him, but he would only step closer and closer. He lacked the sensitivity to see that he was invading my space.

Now, once we're able to withdraw ourselves from the center and create space for another, we must develop the keen sensitivity for just how uniquely different—just how other—our partners are. We tend to see what we have in common; we tend to overlook the differences. When people say, "love is blind," this is what they mean. But true love is not blind. True love is seeing—seeing the differences, the otherness, the good and the bad. True love is seeing and still loving. In Hebrew, the verb "to see" is directly related to the verb "to respect." And that is what seeing with the eyes of true love means. True love requires that we see and accept and respect those we love for who they are, without projecting our dreams and fantasies upon them. This is very hard; because we tend to want to fit those we love into our imaginary pictures of love. And if they don't quite fit, we want to alter them to fit. But if we succeed in seeing not just what we have in common with those we love, but what makes us different, and if we appreciate and honor those differences, then we can take the next step toward giving of ourselves to that person. And simultaneously we must enable our partners to do the same for us, which means allowing them to make a space in their lives for us, allowing them to acknowledge our otherness, allowing them to give of themselves to us.

It's like hugging. When you hug another person you create a space with your arms to include him or her. But, of course, it must be in a manner which allows that person the freedom of opening his or her arms to include you. If that simultaneous giving and receiving doesn't happen, the relationship can't work. It is not love. It is something else, and the something else only creates friction and unhappiness, and eventually the relationship breaks up.

Love is giving of one's self to another. That is what the Kabbalistic story is telling us. The endless light of G-d is endless love, and creation was and continues to be an act of love. The breaking of the vessels represents our inability to independently receive the light of love. And the mending of the vessels is the challenging process of rebuilding ourselves within relationships, so that together we can receive and enjoy the endless light of love.

The 4 habits of highly effective lovers are:
1. Making space (and time) in your life for others
2. Respecting their unique otherness
3. Giving of yourself to them
4. Letting them love you and do the same

An excerpt from *Endless Light* by Rabbi David Aaron
Reprinted with permission of the author

Love

by **Rabbi Adin Steinsaltz**

The word "love" is used in a multitude of contexts, with a myriad of connotations, embracing a wide range of emotions, from the most trivial whim to the most sublime philosophical idea. We all think we know what love means, but precisely because the word is used so often, and in so many ways, it has become fuzzy, obscure, even meaningless. Love of God, love of one's country, love of a spouse, love of children, and love of herring may all be called "love," but they are clearly not the same feeling. Even the expression "making love" refers to an act that does not necessarily have anything to do with love, or, for that matter, any other emotion.

The word "love" is used and misused in so many ways. It refers to emotions that range from the very low to the very high, and may differ considerably in intensity: from a rather weak inclination to an overwhelming passion. Therefore, it is necessary to begin our discussion with the simplest and broadest definition.

The very first element in any kind of love is caring about something. There cannot be love when one does not care. The real opposite of love is not hate, but indifference. The emotions of love and hate do indeed pull in opposite directions; while love means being drawn toward the object of our emotions, hatred is pulling away from it. Yet both love and hate begin with caring. The emotion may not be constant; it may vacillate between love and hate, but the core feeling is, fundamentally, one of caring, of being involved. Only when one is involved can an emotion—positive or negative—develop. It therefore happens that people have ambivalent feelings of love and hate mingled together

In many cases, the emotional involvement may reverse: passionate love may sometimes turn into passionate hate, as happens in cases of disappointment in love. Jealousy is another common case of deep love that has turned into fierce hatred. As the verse in the Song of Songs (8:6) puts it, "Love is strong as death; jealousy is cruel as the grave." It may happen in the opposite direction as well, with hatred turning into love. In any case, the emotion depends on caring about something. On the other hand, when one no longer cares, the object becomes insignificant, and is neither loved nor hated. Indifference is the death of any emotional bond.

Caring is the foundation of love, but it is not the emotion itself. Caring about anything may develop in directions other than love. It may turn into respect or admiration, as happens sometimes when one deals with important people or significant subjects. Thus, one may respect the science of biophysics, or admire a great philosopher. This results in a certain emotional response, but that response will not be love. On the other hand, one may care about something that is dangerous or harmful: an abyss alongside a road, or a tiger on the way. There will be an emotional response—fear, and an attempt to avoid the danger—but it will not be hatred.

Love begins when this caring is not only an objective appraisal, but becomes a personal attachment, when the object is not just "a thing" or "a person" that is judged by itself, but when one becomes involved in the relationship. Certain physical attributes, as well as some mental and emotional responses, are found among people everywhere. A certain amount of caring seems to be inherent in our existence. Love, however, seems to be on a different plane; it seems that love is something that people have to learn. As children develop, first they know and care only about themselves, because they do not really have a clear notion of "outside." As they grow, they begin to find the other, first as a reflection of their own image, then as a separate entity. When they see a creature that is different from themselves, yet somewhat similar, they begin to have a relationship; they begin to care for the other.

The capacity for love may be inborn, but it does not always develop. It may take time and experience until it happens. Caring may develop into compassion—which literally means to feel passion together with another. When compassion grows, the emotional involvement deepens, and then becomes the emotion of love.

Love, then, is the emotion of attraction toward an object—the beloved. But this feeling of attraction is not a single, well-defined emotion. Because of the great variety in personalities, the differences in the object of

love, and the vagueness of the term, there may be many different relationships that people will call "love."

There is a Jewish folk tale that illustrates how vague the meaning of the word "love" can be, and also it demonstrates some of the basic problems in statements such as "I love you." Once upon a time, a fisherman caught a large pike, and when he pulled the fish out of the water and saw its size, he said, "This is wonderful! I'll take it to the Baron; he loves pike." The poor fish says to himself, "There's some hope for me yet." The fisherman brings the fish to the manor house, and the guard says, "What do you have?" "A pike." "Great," says the guard. "The Baron loves pike." The fish feels that there is some corroboration of the facts. The fisherman enters the palace; and though the fish can hardly breathe, he still has hope: the Baron loves pike. He is brought into the kitchen, and all the cooks exclaim how much the Baron loves pike. The fish is placed on a table, and the Baron himself enters, and gives instructions, "Cut off the tail, cut off the head, and slit it this way." With his last breath, the fish cries out in great despair, "Why did you lie? You don't love pike, you love yourself!"

The poor fish clearly had a linguistic-philological problem. It confused two different meanings of the same verb. This raises the question: are these two meanings really so different from each other? Don't people make the same mistake when they think and talk about love? There is "fish love," and there is Love. Clearly, they are not the same. They do not have the same emotional impact, and what is more important, the emotions themselves are not the same.

The various kinds of love differ both in quantity—namely, in how strong and compelling the emotion is—and, more significantly, in quality. Different loves are distinguished from one another by the object of love, and by the feeling itself. Usually, people instinctively differentiate between the different kinds of love, but when they do mix them up, it may become ridiculous, bizarre, and even perverse. A person who is in love will frequently form an attachment to objects that belong to the beloved as well. However, when the emotion toward the beloved's shoe becomes identical to the emotion toward the person, there is a clear case of perversion (fetishism, to use the clinical term). If one loves children in the same way one loves a spouse (or vice versa), this, too, is obviously a mental illness.

With all the emotional differences among the various "loves," they have many things in common. In every love there is strong positive feeling and deep attraction to the beloved, whether it is a person, an idea, or an inanimate object. What "fish love" and Love have in common—in fact, what every form of love has, from the most exalted to the most prosaic—are three components: the subject (the lover), an emotion (love), and an object (the beloved). The nature of the love depends on each of them alone, and on the interrelationships among them. The most exalted kind of love is something that most people can speak about only theoretically. Poets and philosophers write about it, people in love speak about it, and many others yearn for it, but most of us have never experienced it. It is a love that is entirely object-oriented; the lover does not care what benefit or enjoyment he gains from the beloved. The emotional drive, as well as the joy of that love, is in the feeling of love itself. I love something, and I love it as it is, just because it is. I do not need to possess it, or even to have a response from my beloved. Sometimes, the only wish of the lover is just to be as close as possible to the beloved. In higher forms, even this desire does not occur, because the love is just the joy that the beloved exists, and that is enough.

One example of this love may be admiring a beautiful mountain. I do not care whether the mountain responds, whether the mountain loves me back. I also do not want to take it with me. I leave it as it is. I can admire it, I can even experience an intense feeling of love, but I have no desire to possess it, nor do I expect it to give me anything in return.

In most cases, however, love is not so "detached." If I love flowers, and I find a beautiful flower, how should I best express that feeling: by picking it, or by letting it be? If I really love the flower in itself and for itself, the beauty of it, the smell of it, then I should leave it as it is. That would be object-oriented love. However, most people would pick the flower, which means that they not only want to love it, but also to possess it. They are willing to destroy the flower in order to enjoy it. That is also love, but of another kind; it is clearly a subject-oriented love.

The difference between object-oriented and subject-oriented love can be very subtle. Complicating the issue is the fact that anything is liable to become "misused" as the subject of subject-oriented love. In the fish story, it is clear that the Baron's love of pike is completely selfish, and that he cares nothing for the fish, its welfare or its life. He just likes (or even passionately loves) the taste of the fish, because he loves himself, and one of his ways of satisfying that love is by eating the fish. When it comes to human relationships that are more complex, it is not always that clear. Whatever the object of love may be, the question is always: what do I love? Do I really love the object, or do I love myself, and just want to gratify my desires by means of the object?

This problem is very well recognized in the realm of erotic or sensual love. Does one really love the beloved as a person, or is the love only a pretext to have sex with another, enjoying oneself by means of the other, a true "fish love"? There are far more subtle cases. For instance, some people say they love their children, but in truth, they use the youngsters for their own enjoyment. This enjoyment may not necessarily be physical; perhaps they like meddling with another person's life, or having somebody to pet. Either way, it is themselves they care for, not the children. If I need an object, and I keep it in order to meet my needs, I am not really interested in the object, I am just interested in its usefulness to me. Whether the enjoyment is spiritual or material, whether it is simply possessiveness, or gross physical abuse for the sake of enjoyment—if it is about what the object provides for the subject, it is not ideal, selfless love.

This way of probing into the nature of love may become very disturbing. Self-interest may persist from the grossest material benefit to very refined and spiritual forms. One should ask, "How much of my love is simply self-gratification?" It is possible for love of God to be the same as love of pike, e.g., when religiosity is based on one's needs for security, as a crutch for a failing individual, or mostly when it is centered on "what will I get from it."

In every "I love you," whoever or whatever the love and the "you" are, there is, always an "I." A self must always be involved in the process; the emotion of love cannot exist without a self. Even when love requires great self-denial, it still requires a self at the center of the emotion.

It is impossible for love to be entirely devoid of self, because somebody has to be the carrier, the feeler of the emotion.

Indeed, the quality of the emotion of love, the feeling, depends as much upon the subject, the personality of the lover, as upon the object. Some personalities are fiery: their emotion has to rise to higher and higher levels. Others do not have any need for storms; they even prefer a quiet life. Indeed, Jewish sources describe these two kinds of loves as "love like fire" and "love like water."[1] "Love like fire" consumes, it burns a person, while "love like water" is satisfying, soothing.

At first glance, it may seem that the "love like fire" is desire, and "love like water" is fulfillment, but that is not necessarily so; there is a difference in the nature of the emotion itself. A lover consumed with "love like fire" may burn with a compelling need to do something about that love; it makes the lover less and less happy—consumed, but not happy, not joyful. To express their love, some have to shower the beloved with gifts—not in order to bribe or possess the beloved, but as an expression of their burning desire. Yet the more they express it, the more the desire grows. In a sense, those gifts have less to do with the recipient than with the giver: the giver has the satisfaction of giving, of expressing love.[2] Martyrdom is the ultimate expression of love that cannot be satisfied until it is sacrificial, because it is an all-consuming feeling. In contrast, in "love like water," the very existence of the beloved is enough to make the lover happy.

Just as the personality of the lover affects the nature of the love, the object of the love is also essential to the relationship. Not all beloveds lend themselves to the same kind of love; some objects, almost by their very nature, can only be loved in one form and not in another. Loving a beautiful thing and loving food are not the same kind of love; the beautiful object and the food are utilized in different ways.

Some people are so in love with money that they have an almost physical craving for it. The miser who will not use his money derives immense satisfaction just from knowing that he has it. In that case, the money becomes an abstract ideal. One might say that the miser's love is a very delicate kind of love; he does not need anything from his beloved, he does not use his beloved; he is just happy that it is there for him. I once heard about a miserly old man who had a young girl living with him. Everybody told him that it was not him she loved, but his money. To this the miser retorted, "I spent my whole life making money, thinking about money; that was the only thing that really interested me. What am I? I am my money. If she loves the money, she loves me dearly." He identified so with his money that it was no longer just something that he possessed; it was his very self.

The sages of the Talmud differentiate between conditional and unconditional love.[3] In conditional love, fulfillment often results in the end of love. Amnon, the son of King David, fell madly in love with his half-sister Tamar. He tricked her into coming to his bedroom, and despite her pleas, he raped her. "Afterward, Amnon hated her with an intense hatred; he hated her with a hatred even greater than his former love," and he threw her out of his house. This example—a particular historical instance of something that happens frequently—shows how people may deceive even themselves by confusing emotions. Amnon thought that he loved the girl, while in truth he just had a very intense sexual desire. He really wanted something very concrete, and once he got it, Tamar became like a used rag for him: ugly, dirty, and not worth keeping.[4]

Amnon's "love" was clearly conditional. In other cases, however, differentiating between love for a quality or attribute of the beloved, and a higher, more refined love for the person or object, may be a far more delicate matter. If I love someone because he or she is beautiful, clever, powerful, or has some other quality, is it the person that I care about, or is it the quality? Does love connect to an essential self in the beloved, or just to a list of attributes? The question goes even further than that: does love require attributes in the beloved in

---

[1] The Tanya (the fundamental book of Chabad, written by the founder of Chabad, Rabbi Shneur Zalman of Lyady), Chapter 9, and many other writings by the same author.

[2] Indeed, one of the differences between giving charity and giving out of love is that charity is object-oriented; it is connected, or should be connected, with the needs of the recipient.

[3] *Pirkei Avot* ("The Ethics of Our Fathers") 5:16.

[4] See 2 Samuel 13:1–19.

order to exist? Is love rational, at least in the sense that it increases as the attributes get better, more beautiful, more bountiful, more anything? Or is love blind?

It seems that there does not have to be any real connection between the emotion of love and the object of love. Consider the most common kind of love: self-love. Of course, this love is usually quite different from falling in love with another person. Except for pathological cases (extreme narcissism), it does not include any fiery emotion. Still, it has all the elements of love: the attachment, the involvement, the desire to grant the beloved (oneself, that is) every whim, and so on. Because we are born with it, there is no strong emotional display, very much like love within the family; yet it is a very stable and enduring love.

Self-love provides powerful evidence of two important, broadly applicable aspects of love. First, love is blind—or, better yet, hallucinatory. Most people love themselves even though they know more derogatory things about themselves than anybody else could ever find out. In most cases, self-love is a full-fledged, everlasting love affair, and, although it sometimes grows and sometimes diminishes, it exists independently of any special attributes.

Similarly, when I adore a person, a thing, a picture, or an abstract notion, I may be mistaken; I may be blinded by emotion, prejudice, or a chemical reaction. Nevertheless, as long as the imaginary quality exists for me, as long as I see it, the feeling lasts. The imaginary beauty is beautiful, as long as I imagine it to be so. People who fall in love become blind; they do not see the crooked nose or the terrible mental qualities of the beloved. In this case, beauty is indeed in the eye of the beholder. To the male warthog, the female warthog possesses every kind of beauty. It is only when the illusion stops that one realizes there was no substance there, that one loved an illusion, without valid grounds to base it on.

The second aspect of love epitomized by self-love is forgiveness. Even people who are not forgiving—by religion or by temperament—are ready to forgive themselves, and forget almost everything. Forgiveness does not mean that people ignore all their own flaws, but they are able to go on loving themselves, even with all the faults

and all the guilt. How does this happen? At a certain point, when people begin to develop a sense of self, they fall in love with this self, and they cease to demand anything of it; its mere existence is enough for them. Love rarely distorts facts; it covers up faults by changing our estimation of them. Facts somehow do not sound the same, or matter quite as much, when they are about me.

When I love someone, whether it is my child, my spouse, or any other person, I may see the whole person, including the faults, but I just do not care about these faults. In a sense, it is like looking at an airplane propeller. As long as it is moving very fast, one cannot see the blades; once one begins to see them, it means that the propeller is no longer functioning. As long as one looks at the object of love and sees no flaws—just, perhaps, a little blur—then everything is all right. When one begins to focus on details, the appreciation of the whole person is lost, and the love can no longer override the flaws.

A loftier instance of love, however, is described in the Book of Genesis (29: 20): "Jacob worked to get Rachel for seven years, and they were like several days in his eyes, because of his love for her." At first glance, that seems paradoxical—not just because seven years is a long time, but because when one in love is separated from the beloved, a day seems like a year. Yet here, it says just the opposite: seven years was like several days.

If the love of the other is for one's own satisfaction, then being separated from the object of love causes suffering; the more intense the feeling, the longer, subjectively, time seems. When I truly love the other just because the beloved exists, not because I want anything, then seven years and three days are exactly the same. What I get from the love is the love itself. What matters is the relationship, not the benefits derived from it. My beloved exists, and therefore all is well; I need nothing more, not a smile or a look in return for my love. I do not even need my beloved to notice me. Theoretically, the greater love, the more it is centered on the object and the less it has to do with the subject. Ideal love is concentrated on the beloved and nowhere else; the lover feels love, and does not require anything in return.

The loftiest kind of love, the love of God, is described in the Book of Job (13:15). It says there: "Even when He kills me, I still yearn for Him." When I am aware that You, God, are there, everything is all right—not because the world is perfect, or all is well with my life, or because this makes me richer or happier. Life is all right because You exist, and that in itself provides all the satisfaction I need. Job's extreme statement defines the most unconditional kind of love

Some people are born with a great gift for love, while others have to learn love from the very basics—possibly expanding self-love into love for others. For others yet, love is a very difficult exercise, and in order to achieve it, even to the smallest degree, they have to make deep structural personality changes. Some people experience love only for a fleeting moment. Only a few—possibly, those who have this gift from birth—are willing, and able, to attain totally unconditional love.

Simple Words: Thinking About What Really Matters in Life
[New York: Simon & Schuster Paperbacks, 1999], 187–200
Reprinted with permission of the author

When "We" Means "You"

by **Herb Keinon**

"Why do you say 'we,' when you really mean 'me'—that I should get the car washed?" The Wife asked, rather annoyed.

With Purim behind us and Pesach right up ahead, I thought I was being the responsible adult when I mentioned to The Wife last week that we should get the car cleaned before the onset of the great pre-Pesach rush at the local car wash.

But I was wrong.

"Why do you say 'we,' when you really mean 'me'—that I should get the car washed?" she asked, rather annoyed.

"Well, Honey, you know how it is. Half the country vacuums a year's worth of crumbs out of their cars a couple of days before Pesach, and because everyone waits until the last minute, everyone ends up spending about three hours in line, ready to pounce on anyone who looks even remotely like they might jump in front of them.

"Besides, the price for a car wash is always jacked way up right before the holiday. I thought if we get it done now, we won't have to worry about it later."

"But why do you say 'we,' when you really mean 'me,'" she said again, obviously missing my very well-thought-out and considerate point.

So I repeated the point again, using other illustrations of how there are certain things in this country—like buying school books, purchasing a lulav and etrog, or going kayaking up north—that everyone does at the exact same time of year, leading to an unpleasant experience of long lines and short tempers.

"Trust me," The Wife replied. "I know what you're talking about. But don't say 'we,' because you don't mean 'we.' This isn't the royal we, and you're not Prince William. You mean me, that I should do it. Say what you mean. Communicate. Be direct. Don't manipulate."

The Wife then launched into a litany of times when I said "we," but actually meant her.

"Why do you say 'we' should call the new neighbors and invite them for Shabbat, when you mean that I should do it?" she said.

"Why do you say 'we' should call the electric company to straighten out a bill, when you mean I should do it? And why do you say 'we' should go grocery shopping because we're out of milk, when you obviously have no intention in the world of doing it yourself?"

Hmm, interesting points those, albeit a bit troubling. After nearly 25 years of marriage—our anniversary is in a week—The Wife was on to me.

See what a quarter of a century can do?

"I dunno," I said, my eyes downcast. "I guess it's just a manner of speaking."

No, saying "dunno" instead of "don't know" is a manner of speaking, she said. Saying "pop" instead of "soda" is a manner of speaking. Talking with a southern accent is a manner of speaking. What I was doing, she insisted, was bucking responsibility.

Language, indeed, is a marvel: The switching of one small pronoun provides enormous cover. "We should do the dishes" sounds so much better, so less demanding, so less threatening, so much more magnanimous, so much more 21st century husband than "you should do the dishes."

Besides, I argued, having been married for so long, having shared so much, having raised four children and having gone through the proverbial thick and thin, we were a unit, flesh of one flesh and all that.

"We, me, you. What's the difference, really? We are one," I said, sounding like an advertisement for the Greater Boston Jewish Federation.

Twenty-five years is, indeed, a long time. It's funny how one's concept of time changes. I remember in college when my folks celebrated their 25th anniversary thinking that 25 years was an eternity, and wondering how it was possible to wake up to the same person for so long.

Those were the days when I also wondered how one could keep one job longer than the three months of summer vacation. And then—boom—there I am on the same playing field.

These romantic we-are-one musings, however, were interrupted when The Wife raised an even more salient and disturbing point: How could it be, she asked, if I professed to love her so dearly, that I would want to dump all those little things I hated doing precisely onto her? Why indeed? I mean, would Romeo ask Juliet to clean the balcony? Would Woody Allen ask Soon-Yi Previn to clean his glasses? Would Homer Simpson ask Marge Bouvier to clean the chickens (well, he probably would).

My first instinct was to say that this was just the way I was wired, what I picked up from my surroundings. But I knew this deterministic explanation would not fly with The Wife, who also happens to be a psychotherapist.

No, that explanation was too easy and superficial. I was going to have to delve deep down and comb the inner chambers of my soul to come up with a better answer than that.

And while I was down there delving around, she said, I should try to figure out why I do the same thing to the sweet, unsuspecting children, like asking them to go borrow things from the neighbors—something I loathe and adamantly refuse to do.

"Perhaps it's because you, and the kids, don't mind doing these things as much as I do," I spurted out, thinking of the time when we were courting and The Wife (then The Girlfriend) said she'd do the dishes, and that she actually liked doing the dishes because she found it relaxing.

"Wow, this is going to be great," I had thought, only to learn soon after that she didn't mean it, and that the things I disliked, she disliked as well—which is actually one of the reasons we have proven to be so compatible.

"Or perhaps," I said, "there is a streak of selfishness that runs through us all, and we would rather have someone else do something aggravating, in order to save ourselves the aggravation."

Finally, she smiled. And then she asked when "we" were going to plan a getaway for our anniversary.

I got on it the next day.

Jerusalem Post, March 27, 2011
Reprinted with permission of the publisher

Lesson 4
Becoming a Better Half
What is a *Mensch*?

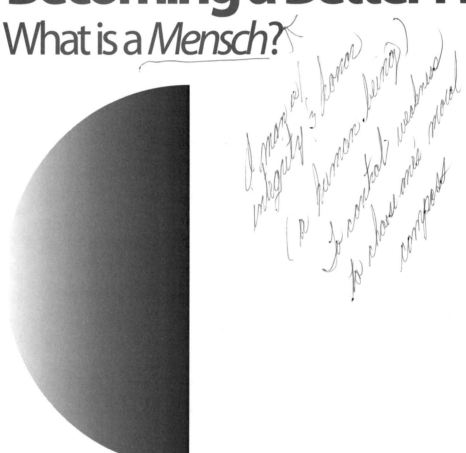

a marvel, integrity & honor
(a human being)
to control weakness
to choose one's moral compass

Introduction

Marriage can bring out the best and worst in us. By challenging us in our weakest areas, our relationship can be a catalyst for developing new strengths and a better personality.

Marriage Material
Humanism vs. Determinism

Text 1 ▮

Rabbi Shne'ur Zalman of Liadi (1745–1812). Chasidic rebbe and founder of the Chabad movement, also known as "the Alter Rebbe" and "the Rav." Born in Liozna, Belarus, he was among the principal students of the Magid of Mezeritch. His numerous works include the *Tanya*, an early classic containing the fundamentals of Chasidism; *Torah Or; Likutei Torah*; and *Shulchan Aruch HaRav*, a reworked and expanded code of Jewish law. He is interred in Hadich, Ukraine, and was succeeded by his son, Rabbi Dovber of Lubavitch.

המוח שליט על הלב בתולדתו וטבע יצירתו. שכך נוצר האדם בתולדתו, שכל אדם יכול ברצונו שבמוחו להתאפק ולמשול ברוח תאותו שבלבו שלא למלאת משאלות לבו במעשה דבור ומחשבה

תניא, פרק יב

The mind rules over the instincts by virtue of a human's inborn nature. Employing the willpower of the mind, people can restrain themselves and control the drives of the heart, preventing the heart's desires from manifesting in action, word, or thought.

Rabbi Shne'ur Zalman of Liadi, *Tanya*, ch. 12

Text 2

Viktor Emil Frankl, MD, PhD (1905–1997). Professor of neurology and psychiatry at the University of Vienna Medical School and founder of the psychotherapeutic school called logotherapy. During World War II he spent three years in various concentration camps, including Theresienstadt, Auschwitz, and Dachau. Frankl authored 39 books, which have been published in 38 languages. His most famous book, *Man's Search for Meaning,* has sold over 9 million copies in the U.S. alone.

We who lived in concentration camps can remember the men who walked through the huts comforting others, giving away their last piece of bread. They may have been few in number, but they offer sufficient proof that everything can be taken from a man but one thing: the last of the human freedoms—to choose one's attitude in any given set of circumstances, to choose one's own way.

Viktor Frankl, *Man's Search for Meaning* [New York: Simon & Schuster, 1984], p. 86

Text 3 🔖

What is the Torah definition of a human? A human has the capacity for self-assessment. A human has the mental and moral capacity to override impulse (can a dog decide to go on a diet?). A human can choose to follow his moral compass instead of his physical inclination. A human can calculate consequences beyond the immediate. That is the Torah description of a human, the Torah definition of a *mensch*. . . .

So the Torah definition of "human" is something we should all strive for.

Interestingly, the term has different connotations when used in American parlance. When a person is weak, less than noble, impulse-driven instead of morally focused, what do we say?

"Listen, he's only human!"

In our vernacular, recognizing that a person is "human" is acknowledging his inherent weakness. We see a human as inherently flawed and morally feeble. We cut a guy slack because we know he can't reach a noble goal; after all, he's only human! What can you really expect from this person of flesh and blood?

Think about it. The Torah/Jewish term of human—*mensch*—is something to strive for, while the American "human" is a fall-back position in case of moral failure.

Rabbi Mendy Herson, "On Being a *Mensch*," www.chabad.org

Rabbi Mendy Herson (1967–). Director of the Chabad Jewish Center in Basking Ridge, New Jersey, and associate dean at the Rabbinical College of America.

The Voice of Choice

Text 4

וַיִּיצֶר ה' אֱלֹקִים אֶת הָאָדָם עָפָר מִן הָאֲדָמָה, וַיִּפַּח בְּאַפָּיו נִשְׁמַת חַיִּים, וַיְהִי הָאָדָם לְנֶפֶשׁ חַיָּה.

בראשית ב,ז

And God formed man from dust of the earth, and He breathed into his nostrils the soul of life, and man became a living spirit.

Genesis 2:7

(a talking soul)

Figure 4.1

Silent (Inanimate)	דּוֹמֵם	*Domem*
Vegetation	צוֹמֵחַ	*Tome'ach*
Life (Animal)	חַי	*Chai*
Articulator (Human)	מְדַבֵּר	*Medaber*

Mineral

Man is the only creation that can behave against its nature

Anger Management
The Danger of Anger

Text 5

Anger is the first emotion that human beings experience, and it is the last one that we learn to manage effectively. As early as four months of age, the human infant's vague feelings of distress differentiate into recognizable anger; for many of us, a lifetime is spent in denying, suppressing, displacing, or avoiding this troublesome emotional experience.

John E. Jones and Anthony G. Banet, Jr., "Dealing with Anger," in *Presentation and Discussion Resources: Communication* [San Francisco: Jossey-Bass/Pfeiffer, 1998], p. 318

Text 6

הכעס מדה רעה היא עד למאד, וראוי לאדם שיתרחק ממנה עד הקצה האחר, וילמד עצמו שלא יכעוס ואפילו על דבר שראוי לכעוס עליו.

משנה תורה, הלכות דעות ב,ג

Anger is an exceptionally bad quality. It is proper to distance oneself from anger to the furthest extreme and train oneself not to become angry even in response to an incident that rightfully calls for anger.

Maimonides, *Mishneh Torah,* Laws of Personal Development 2:3

Rabbi Moshe ben Maimon (1135–1204). Better known as Maimonides or by the acronym Rambam; was born in Cordoba, Spain. After the conquest of Cordoba by the Almohads, he fled Spain and eventually settled in Cairo, Egypt. There, he became the leader of the Jewish community and served as court physician to the vizier of Egypt. His rulings on Jewish law are considered integral to the formation of halachic consensus. He is most noted for authoring the *Mishneh Torah,* an encyclopedic arrangement of Jewish law, and for his philosophical work, *Guide for the Perplexed.*

Question for Discussion

Why is anger anathema to a greater degree than other negative qualities? Is anger ever an appropriate reaction?

Text 7

בשלושה מקומות בא לכלל כעס ובא לכלל טעות.
ספרי, מטות ה

Moses became angry on three occasions, and in each instance he then erred.

Sifrei, Matot 5

Text 8

Studies comparing anger with sadness, worry, or neutral emotion have shown that angry participants make more stereotypic judgments, rely on fewer diagnostic cues, make greater use of chronically accessible scripts, and pay more attention to superficial cues and less attention to the argument quality of persuasive messages. . . . Anger is likely to make criminal investigators rely on superficial processing, and hence base their judgments more on preexisting expectations and beliefs, compared with emotions that prompt deep processing. . . .

[Similarly,] jurors experiencing higher levels of anger were somewhat less likely to accurately report inconsistencies, in line with the idea that anger reduces substantive processing.

Karl Ask and Par Anders Granhag, "Hot Cognition in Investigative Judgments: The Differential Influence of Anger and Sadness," *Law and Human Behavior* 31, no. 6 (2007), pp. 539–540

Karl Ask (1978–). Associate professor of psychology at University of Gothenburg, Sweden, his research interests are in the field of criminal, legal, and investigative psychology.

Par Anders Granhag (1946–). Professor of psychology at University of Gothenburg, Sweden, his research activities build on cognitive psychology with a specific interest in the psychology of criminal investigations and the courtroom.

Personality Analysis

Optional Section

Learning Interaction 1

Rate the following four personality types, from 1 to 4 (1 is the most advantageous, 4 is the least); then suggest an adjective for each of the personality types.

Personality Type	Ranking	Adjective
Difficult to anger and difficult to appease		
Difficult to anger and easy to appease		
Easy to anger and easy to appease		
Easy to anger and difficult to appease		

Text 9a

ארבע מדות בדעות:

נוח לכעוס ונוח לרצות, יצא הפסדו בשכרו.

קשה לכעוס וקשה לרצות, יצא שכרו בהפסדו.

קשה לכעוס ונוח לרצות, חסיד.

נוח לכעוס וקשה לרצות, רשע.

משנה, אבות ה,יא

There are four types of temperaments:

One who is easy to anger and easy to appease—his gain cancels his loss.

One who is difficult to anger and difficult to appease—his loss cancels his gain.

One who is difficult to anger and easy to appease is a pious person.

One who is easy to anger and difficult to appease is wicked.

Mishnah, Avot 5:11

Mishnah. The first authoritative work of Jewish law—in addition to the biblical books—that was codified in writing, it consists of the oral traditions that were passed down from teacher to student. Due to the perpetual persecution of the Jewish people, it became increasingly difficult to guarantee that the oral traditions would not be forgotten. Therefore, Rabbi Yehudah Hanasi, at the end of the second century, redacted the Mishnah.

The Mishnah supplements, complements, clarifies, and systematizes the commandments of the Torah. It is the central literary document that serves as the foundation for both the Jerusalem Talmud and the Babylonian Talmud.

Text 9b

יש בני אדם קשים בטבע, ומפני הקושי שלהם אינם נוחים לכעוס ואינם נוחים לרצות מפני קושיים.

ויש בני אדם שהם רכים בטבע בכל, והם נוחים לכעוס ונוחים לרצות.

כלל הדבר: או שהוא קשה בכל או שהוא רך בכל, ואין הטבע נותן שיהיה נוח לכעוס ויהיה קשה לרצות, שיהיה בו מן שתי המדות . . .

ולפיכך אמר "קשה לכעוס ונוח לרצות, חסיד". דודאי כיון שהוא קשה לכעוס טבעו קשה ומפני כך קשה לכעוס, ומה שהוא נוח לרצות בזה בודאי שהוא אוהב הבריות ולכך הוא נוח לרצות ומתגבר על טבעו. או איפכא, שהוא בטבע רך ולכך הוא נוח לרצות, ומה שהוא קשה לכעוס אין זה רק שגובר על טבעו שלא יכעוס על הבריות מפני אהבת הבריות וחס על כבוד הבריות ולכך הוא חסיד בודאי.

וכן אם הוא נוח לכעוס וקשה לרצות, בודאי או שטבעו בודאי רך ולכך הוא נוח לכעוס, ואם כן למה אינו נוח לרצות? אלא שהוא שונא הבריות ולכך אינו נוח להם לרצות מפני רשעתו. או איפכא שהוא קשה בטבע, ולפיכך הוא קשה לרצות. ואם כן למה אינו קשה לכעוס? רק מפני שהוא שונא את הבריות ולכך הוא נוח לכעוס ולכך הוי רשע.

דרך חיים, שם

There are individuals who are naturally insensitive. Therefore, they are not easy to anger, but are also difficult to appease.

Then there are those who are naturally sensitive, and are therefore easy to anger and easy to appease.

As a general rule, people are either insensitive or sensitive in all areas. It is unnatural, however, for a person to be easy to anger and difficult to appease, for these are two opposing characteristics. . . .

Therefore the *mishnah* says, "One who is difficult to anger and easy to appease is a pious person." For if he is difficult to anger, that is an indication that he is naturally insensitive. The fact, then, that he is easily appeased must be attributed to his love of his fellows, which causes him to overcome his nature and be appeased without great effort. Alternatively, it is possible that he is naturally sensitive, hence he is easily appeasable. The fact, then, that he is difficult to anger is unnatural and must be attributed to his love and respect for his fellows. [Either way,] this is a pious individual.

The opposite is true with regard to one who is easily angered and difficult to appease. One of two possibilities must apply: Perhaps he is naturally sensitive, and therefore is easily angered. If so, why isn't he easy to appease? It must be that due to his contempt for his fellows, he chooses not to be easily appeased. Alternatively, perhaps he is naturally insensitive. If so, why isn't he difficult to anger? It must be that due to his contempt for his fellows, he chooses to be easily angered. [Either way,] this is clearly a wicked person.

Rabbi Yehudah Loew, *Derech Chayim*, ad loc.

Rabbi Yehudah Loew (1525–1609). Talmudist and philosopher, also known as the Maharal of Prague, he descended from the Babylonian exilarchs. Maharal rose to prominence as leader of the famed Jewish community of Prague. He is the author of more than a dozen works of original philosophic thought, most notably *Tiferet Yisrael* and *Netsach Yisrael*. He also authored a commentary on the Talmud, and *Gur Aryeh*, a super-commentary on Rashi's biblical commentary. He is buried in the Old Jewish Cemetery of Prague.

End of Optional Section

Reacting to an Anger-Provoking Situation

Text 10

מעשה בבן שכבד את אביו ביותר. אמר לו אביו, "אתה מכבדיני בחיי, תכבדני במותי.
אני מצוך שתלין כעסך לילה אחד, ועצור רוחך שלא תדבר".
לאחר פטירת אביו הלך למדינת הים, והניח אשתו מעוברת והוא לא ידע, ועכב בדרך
ימים ושנים. וכשחזר בעיר, בא בלילה, ועלה לחדר שאשתו היתה שם שוכבת, ושמע
קולו של בחור שהיה מנשק אותה. שלף חרבו ורצה להרוג שניהם, וזכר מצות אביו
והשיבו לתערה.
שמע שאמרה לאותו בחור, בנה שאצלה, "כבר יש שנים רבות שהלך אביך מאצלי.
אילו היה יודע שנולד לו בן, כבר הגיע להשיא לך אשה".
כששמע זה הדבר אמר, "פתחי לי אחותי רעייתי! ברוך ה' שעצר כעסי, וברוך אבי
שציווני לעצור כעסי כעסי לילה אחד, שלא הרגתי אותך ואת בני".

ספר חסידים, תרנה

There was once a son who had utmost respect for his father. [Before the father passed away,] he told his son, "You have honored me during my lifetime; I hope you will continue to do so after my death [by observing this last instruction]: Always allow a night to pass before you act on your anger; remain quiet and do not respond [until a night has passed]."

After his father's passing, the son traveled overseas, leaving behind a wife who, unbeknownst to him, was pregnant. Due to circumstances, he remained overseas many years. When he returned, he arrived in his city at night. He approached his wife's room, and [from behind the door,] he heard the sound of a young man kissing his wife. He unsheathed his sword and was about to kill them both, when he remembered his father's final instruction, and he returned the sword to its scabbard.

Rabbi Yehudah ben Shmuel Hachasid (1140–1217). Born in Speyer, Germany, he was a rabbi, mystic, and one of the initiators of Chasidei Ashkenaz, a Jewish German moralist movement that stressed piety and asceticism. Rabbi Yehudah settled in Regensburg in 1195. He is best known for his work *Sefer Chasidim*. His most prominent students were Rabbi Elazar Roke'ach and Rabbi Moshe ben Ya'akov of Coucy.

Thereafter he heard his wife telling the young man, "It is already many years that your father is gone. Were he to know that I gave birth to a son, he would certainly come to marry you off."

When the husband heard this, he proclaimed, "Open up for me, my beloved. Blessed is God for tempering my anger, and blessed is my father who instructed me to never act upon my anger until a night has passed. It is thanks to them that I did not kill you and my son!"

Rabbi Yehudah ben Shmuel of Regensburg, *Sefer Chasidim* 655

The Larger Picture

Text 11

Graf Pototcki was the son of a high nobleman, and his conversion to Judaism was a threat to the Church, which condemned him to death if he did not recant. Pototcki fled and lived incognito in a small village, where he spent his time studying Torah. The villagers knew his secret but, of course, would not expose him.

There was a young boy in the village who often harassed him, and Pototcki pleaded with him to desist. The boy told his father that Pototcki had shouted at him and, to retaliate, the father revealed Pototcki's whereabouts to the Church. Pototcki was taken into custody and was told that if he did not retract his conversion, he would be burned at the stake.

Pototcki refused to deny his faith and the cruel execution was carried out, with Pototcki's reciting the Shema with his last breath.

The executioner, seeing that Pototcki was unperturbed by his imminent death, said, "You are no doubt thinking that when you get up to heaven you will bring down the wrath of God on us."

"Not at all," Pototcki said. "When I was a child, I had little clay soldiers with which I played. One young boy was jealous of me and broke my soldiers. I cried to my father and asked him to punish the boy. When my father ignored me, I thought, 'Wait until I grow up and become the local feudal lord. I will then punish this boy.'

"When I grew up and did have the power to punish him, I was mature enough to realize how foolish it was to make an issue of something as insignificant as a few little clay soldiers, and I did nothing to punish the man who had broken them when he was a child.

"When I get to heaven and realize how insignificant is this puny little body that you are about to destroy, do you think I will make an issue of it?"

Rabbi Abraham J. Twerski, *The Enemy Within* [Shaar Press, 2002], pp. 37–38

Rabbi Abraham J. Twerski, MD
(1930–). Born in Milwaukee, scion to the Chernobyl Chasidic dynasty, he is a well-known expert in the field of substance abuse. Rabbi Twerski has authored more than 50 books on self-help and Judaism, and has served a pioneering role in heightening awareness on the issues of addiction, spousal abuse, and low self-esteem. He served as medical director of the Gateway Rehabilitation Center in Pittsburgh, and associate professor of psychiatry at the University of Pittsburgh School of Medicine.

וַיֹּאמֶר ה׳ אֶל מֹשֶׁה: "רָאִיתִי אֶת הָעָם הַזֶּה, וְהִנֵּה עַם קְשֵׁה עֹרֶף הוּא. וְעַתָּה הַנִּיחָה לִּי
וְיִחַר אַפִּי בָהֶם וַאֲכַלֵּם, וְאֶעֱשֶׂה אוֹתְךָ לְגוֹי גָּדוֹל׃"
וַיְחַל מֹשֶׁה אֶת פְּנֵי ה׳ אֱלֹקָיו, וַיֹּאמֶר: "לָמָה ה׳ יֶחֱרֶה אַפְּךָ בְּעַמֶּךָ אֲשֶׁר הוֹצֵאתָ מֵאֶרֶץ
מִצְרַיִם בְּכֹחַ גָּדוֹל וּבְיָד חֲזָקָה? . . . שׁוּב מֵחֲרוֹן אַפֶּךָ וְהִנָּחֵם עַל הָרָעָה לְעַמֶּךָ.
זְכֹר לְאַבְרָהָם לְיִצְחָק וּלְיִשְׂרָאֵל עֲבָדֶיךָ, אֲשֶׁר נִשְׁבַּעְתָּ לָהֶם בָּךְ, וַתְּדַבֵּר אֲלֵהֶם, אַרְבֶּה
אֶת זַרְעֲכֶם כְּכוֹכְבֵי הַשָּׁמַיִם וְכָל הָאָרֶץ הַזֹּאת אֲשֶׁר אָמַרְתִּי אֶתֵּן לְזַרְעֲכֶם וְנָחֲלוּ לְעֹלָם.
וַיִּנָּחֶם ה׳ עַל הָרָעָה אֲשֶׁר דִּבֶּר לַעֲשׂוֹת לְעַמּוֹ׃"

שמות לב,ט-יד

God said to Moses: "I have seen this people and behold, they are a stiff-necked nation! Now leave Me alone; My anger will blaze upon them and I will annihilate them, and I will make you into a great nation."

Moses entreated his God, and said: "Why, O God, should Your anger be directed against Your people whom You have brought out from Egypt with great power and with a strong hand? . . . Turn away from Your fierce anger and reconsider the evil [You intended] for Your people.

"Remember Abraham, Isaac, and Israel, Your servants, to whom You swore by Your very Self and said: 'I will multiply your seed like the stars of the heavens, and all this land that I said I would give to your seed, they shall keep it as their possession forever.'"

God relented and [agreed not to bring] the evil He had said He would [bring] upon His people.

Exodus 32:9–14

Text 12b

כאדם שאומר לחבירו, "למה תקצוף ותאבד לשעה קלה דבר שטרחת בו כמה טורח
והוצאת בו כמה הוצאות?"

רבינו מיוחס בן אליהו, שם

Like a person who tells his friend, "Why get angry and in a heartbeat forfeit that for which you labored and exerted so much effort and into which you invested so much?"

Rabbi Meyuchas ben Eliyahu, ad loc.

Rabbi Meyuchas ben Eliyahu authored a commentary to the Pentateuch that focuses on the simple meaning of the verses. Until the 20th century, this commentary went mostly unnoticed. Not much is known about the author. His writing indicates that he lived in a Greek-speaking country, but it is not clear when. Some suggest he lived as early as the 12th century, while others place him in the latter half of the 15th century.

שׁוּב מֵחֲרוֹן אַפֶּךָ

Who Is in the Picture?

Text 13a

אין אדם רואה חובה לעצמו

תלמוד בבלי, כתובות קה,ב

People do not see their own faults.

Talmud, Ketubot 105b

Babylonian Talmud. A literary work of monumental proportions that draws upon the totality of the legal, spiritual, intellectual, ethical, and historical traditions of Judaism, the Babylonian Talmud was set up as a commentary to the Mishnah and was written primarily in Aramaic. The Talmud contains the teachings of the Jewish sages, mostly from the period after the destruction of the Second Temple through the fifth century C.E. The Babylonian Talmud has served as the primary vehicle for the education of countless Jews over the centuries; it is the entry point for all subsequent legal, ethical, and theological Jewish scholarship.

Question **for Discussion**

Are people really incapable of seeing their own flaws and faults?

Text 13b

"אין אדם רואה חוב לעצמו", אין הפירוש שאינו יודע כלל חובותיו. אדרבה, יוכל
לראות ולהבין היטב עמקות פחיתותו יותר מראיית זולתו עליו, שהרי זולתו אינו רואה
אלא לעינים והוא יראה ללבב.
אלא הכוונה שאין החוב תופס מקום אצלו כלל להתפעל מזה, וכאילו אינו רואה אותו
כלל, כי מפני האהבה הגדולה אשר הוא אוהב מאד את עצמו, על כל פשעיו שיודע
בדעתו תכסה האהבה בבחינת מקיף שלא יומשך מן הידיעה לידי התפעלות במדות,
ולכן אין תופסים מקום כלל להתפעל מזה.
דרך מצותיך, אהבת ישראל כט,א

"**P**eople do not see their own faults" does not mean that people are literally unaware of their own faults. To the contrary, people perceive and understand the depth of their own deficiencies to a far greater degree than others—for others only see that which is visible to the eye, whereas a person alone knows that which transpires in his or her own heart.

Rather, the intent of the statement is that one's own fault is not consequential enough to upset one's equanimity. It is *as if* the faults are invisible, for they are covered by a layer of self-love. [Though intellectually aware of the deficiencies,] the knowledge does not evoke an emotional response, nor does it cause undue concern.

Rabbi Menachem Mendel Schneersohn, *Derech Mitsvotecha, Ahavat Yisrael* 29a

Rabbi Menachem Mendel Schneersohn (1789–1866). Also known as the Tsemach Tsedek, after the title of his compendium of responsa. Third leader of the Chabad Chasidic movement and noted authority on Jewish law and Kabbalah, he was raised by his grandfather, Rabbi Shne'ur Zalman of Liadi, after his mother's passing. Active in the plight of Russian Jewry, he worked to ease the plight of the Cantonists, Jewish children kidnapped and forcibly conscripted to the Czar's army. He is buried in the village of Lubavitch.

Text 14

אורח טוב מהו אומר? "כמה טרחות טרח בעל הבית בשבילי! כמה בשר הביא לפני,
כמה יין הביא לפני, כמה גלוסקאות הביא לפני! וכל מה שטרח לא טרח אלא בשבילי".
אבל אורח רע מהו אומר? "מה טרח בעל הבית זה? פת אחת אכלתי, חתיכה אחת
אכלתי, כוס אחת שתיתי, כל טורח שטרח בעל הבית לא טרח אלא בשביל אשתו
ובניו!"

תלמוד בבלי, ברכות נח,א

What does a good guest say? "How much trouble my host has undergone for me! How much meat he has set before me! How much wine he has set before me! How many cakes he has set before me! And all this trouble was only for my sake!"

What does a bad guest say? "How much, after all, has my host put himself out? I have eaten but one piece of bread and one slice of meat, and drunk but one cup of wine! All the trouble that my host has taken was only for the sake of his wife and children!"

Talmud, Berachot 58a

Text 15

רבי חייא הוה קא מצערא ליה דביתהו. כי הוה משכח מידי, צייר ליה בסודריה ומייתי ניהלה.

אמר ליה רב, "והא קא מצערא ליה למר!"

אמר ליה, "דיינו שמגדלות בנינו, ומצילות אותנו מן החטא".

תלמוד בבלי, יבמות סג,א–ב

Rabbi Chiya was constantly tormented by his wife. [Nevertheless,] whenever he happened upon anything [suitable for a gift], he would wrap it in his kerchief and bring it to her.

Rav said to him, "But she is tormenting you!"

"It is sufficient for us," Rabbi Chiya replied, "that they raise our children and deliver us from sin."

Talmud, Yevamot 63a–b

Text 16

האדם נפעל כפי פעולותיו, ולבו וכל מחשבותיו תמיד אחר מעשיו שהוא עושה בהם, אם טוב ואם רע . . . כי אחרי הפעולות נמשכים הלבבות.

ספר החינוך, מצוה טז

People are impacted by their behaviors. Feelings and thoughts are always a corollary of action, for good or for bad. . . . The heart is drawn in the wake of the deed.

Sefer Hachinuch, Mitzvah 16

Sefer Hachinuch is a work on the 613 commandments, arranged in the order of the *mitzvot's* appearance in the Torah. Four aspects of every mitzvah are discussed in this work: the definition of the mitzvah and its sources in the Written and Oral Torah; ethical lessons that can be deduced from the mitzvah; basic laws pertaining to the observance of the mitzvah; and who is obligated to perform the mitzvah and when. The work was composed in the 13th century by an anonymous author who refers to himself in the introduction as "the Levite of Barcelona." It has been widely thought that this referred to Rabbi Aharon Halevi of Barcelona (Re'ah); however, this view has been contested.

Key Points

1. The greatest qualitative difference between humans and all other creations is the capacity to act in a manner that is antithetical to their natural instincts.

2. The human ability to maintain relationships, and specifically the marital relationship, stems from the capacity to control natural impulses. The more we master this art, the deeper and better our relationships will be.

3. Our sages tell us to avoid anger at all costs, even when it is the logically appropriate reaction. This is because anger spawns many other faults.

4. One should never act upon anger until one is aware of all the pertinent facts, for it is possible that vital qualifying information is missing.

5. Much anger and anguish can be prevented if we adopt a broader outlook. Even if an action warrants anger, one should ask whether it is consequential in the bigger picture.

6. People do not define themselves based on their own faults, instead viewing them as challenges that require addressing. The same attitude should be incorporated in one's reaction to a spouse's faults.

7. Appreciation results from one's choice to focus on the good that the other provides, even if that good is seemingly self-serving.

8. Considering that people are incomplete without their spouse, a spouse deserves appreciation just for "being."

Take-Home Exercise

The following appreciation exercise is from *The Seven Principles for Making Marriage Work* by John M. Gottman and Nan Silver.[1] This is a great exercise to do with your spouse—even if your marriage is stable and happy—and makes for a fun and constructive weekly or bi-weekly activity.

"I Appreciate . . ."

From the list on the following page, circle three items that you think are characteristic of your partner. If there are more than three, still circle just three. (You can circle another three if you choose to do this exercise again.) If you're having difficulty coming up with three, feel free to define the word *characteristic* very loosely. Even if you can recall only one instance when your partner displayed this characteristic, you can circle it.

---

[1] New York: Crown Publishers, 1999, pp. 68–69.

1. Loving	25. Cheerful	49. Nurturing
2. Sensitive	26. Coordinated	50. Warm
3. Brave	27. Graceful	51. Virile
4. Intelligent	28. Elegant	52. Kind
5. Thoughtful	29. Gracious	53. Gentle
6. Generous	30. Playful	54. Practical
7. Loyal	31. Caring	55. Lusty
8. Truthful	32. A great friend	56. Witty
9. Strong	33. Exciting	57. Relaxed
10. Energetic	34. Thrifty	58. Beautiful
11. Sexy	35. Full of plans	59. Handsome
12. Decisive	36. Shy	60. Rich
13. Creative	37. Vulnerable	61. Calm
14. Imaginative	38. Committed	62. Lively
15. Fun	39. Involved	63. A great partner
16. Attractive	40. Expressive	64. A great parent
17. Interesting	41. Active	65. Assertive
18. Supportive	42. Careful	66. Protective
19. Funny	43. Reserved	67. Sweet
20. Considerate	44. Adventurous	68. Tender
21. Affectionate	45. Receptive	69. Powerful
22. Organized	46. Reliable	70. Flexible
23. Resourceful	47. Responsible	71. Understanding
24. Athletic	48. Dependable	72. Totally silly

For each item you checked, briefly think of an actual incident that illustrates this characteristic of your partner. Write the characteristic and the incident in your notebook or journal as follows:

1. Characteristic:

Incident:

---

2. Characteristic:

Incident:

---

3. Characteristic:

Incident:

Now share your list with your partner. Let him or her know what it is about these traits that you value so highly.

Additional Readings

Anger

by **Jay Litvin**

You wanna know about anger? I'll tell you about anger. That's all I can do. I can tell you about it. And then you do what you want. Or what you can. Because anger will ruin your whole stinking life, if you let it. And maybe even if you don't. Anger, my friend, is one tough cookie. It grabs you. Twists you. Overcomes you. And then goes about destroying the things you love best in your whole life.

That's anger.

It grips you in the middle of your chest. Your chest feels tight. What you're feeling is the resistance of your flesh and muscle and bone against a pressure, an energy, an evil excitement that is bursting to get out. It's stronger than you, buddy. You have to know that. It's stronger and when it can't burst out of your chest or squeeze through the spaces of your rib cage or rip your heart into little pieces, it finds another route. It starts to flow out to your arms, up into your head. It hits the muscles in your shoulders and makes them tense and tight and ready to strike out. It makes your arms tingle and your tendons rigid. Your whole neck goes hard as the anger begins to flood your brain.

Sure you try to stop it. But this makes you even more tense, more frustrated, as you now begin to feel like the victim of this surge of fury. The anger's got you. You're angry that you're angry. You're feeling helpless against the uncontrollable urge. And as it fills your mind you're losing your power to resist it. Because now it's got your rational self in its jaws and its making mincemeat out of your attempts at logic and understanding.

Now, my friend, watch as your thoughts turn black and accusing. Watch how the anger has not only conquered your mind but now has your mind colluding with the anger. Fueling it. Thoughts that won't go away. Accusations. Blame. Indignation. Guilt. Jealousy. Hurt feelings. Scars and old wounds enflamed and enflaming.

And now comes the test: Will you act or not? Will you speak or not? Will you yell and hurt, insult and accuse? Will you trash and destroy? Will you lie and manipulate?

Will you begin to destroy your life and all the things you hold so dear?

An exaggeration? Not by a long shot. Because anger can destroy in a flash or over time. Even after all the I'm-sorry's and forgive-me's, even after you've made up and are trying to put it back the way it was, even after the flood of warmth that often follows after you've cooled-down, the damage has been done. And the damage can be forever.

Year after year, outburst after outburst, chink by chink you are destroying something that you once cherished, and maybe still do. You'll notice, if you have that much awareness left, that there's not as much trust as you once enjoyed, not as much openness. Not as much love.

I'm an expert on anger. I've lived with it all my life.

My anger has caused me and others irrevocable harm. I've tried countless ways to get a hold on my anger, but nothing seemed to work. The strength of the emotion was such that no techniques could quell its outburst. And it seemed that no matter how hard I tried to understand the source of this anger—whether in the past or the present—and to erase or correct it—I could not stem its destructive outbreak.

Anger, despite its destructiveness, holds pleasure, a surge of energy that enlivens the life of one whose life has grown dull. There is the righteousness—the sense of justice and punishment. The victory—not allowing one's loss or defeat to go without response. The vengeance—for the wrongs of yesterday or today. The simple feeling of strength and power, the sense of control, the gratification of seeing fear in the eyes of another rather than feel it in oneself.

And, of course, there is the delight of release and the relaxation that comes after one's fury is spent. And often there is the softening, the opening of the heart that had been so imprisoned in bonds of frustration and hurt, old and current, real and imagined. There is the desire for forgiveness and reconciliation, even the pleasure of guilt and remorse that follows.

The pleasure inherent in anger is the source of its sin. The destructiveness becomes simply the price of the pleasure, and the pleasure—like an addiction—is craved after and uncontrollable. Like envy or jealousy or greed or gossip it is nearly impossible to control, so powerful is the satisfaction and fulfillment it brings.

But if one is very lucky—for in the end I think it is primarily good fortune and Divine grace that overcomes anger—one gets to see that there is a different kind of pleasure, one that comes from kindness and forbearance, understanding and forgiveness, and, in simple terms, the pleasure that comes from having peace in the home and between humans, especially humans that you love.

And once you have the good fortune to see or experience this, well, this pleasure so out-intensifies the pleasure from anger that you simply don't want to waste your time. Because, you see, anger is a luxury for those who believe they have time.

But time is an illusion. Time is here only now. And once you realize this, you get to make a decision about how you want to spend your now. Especially when you know that it is the only now you have and may ever have.

Do you really want to spend it in anger and create all that destruction?

Now, don't get me wrong. When I say that overcoming anger is primarily a matter of luck or good fortune, I am not saying that one who is afflicted with uncontrollable anger (is there any other kind?) shouldn't do,

as I did, everything that he or she can to get it under control, whether that be therapy, meditation, jogging or whatever. Though it may be luck and Divine grace that finally brings the desired outcome, in the meantime the responsibility for anger and its consequences lies entirely with me and you.

And when I say that no techniques worked for me, I could just as easily say that all have worked for me, for I have literally spent decades working on this unfortunate part of myself in the hope of ending the spiral of destruction and loss of trust that anger brings in its wake. I look at this work as an investment, as seeding the field knowing that in the end it is only G-d that determines when and whether the crops will grow. In the meantime it is up to us to plough, seed and pray, plough, seed and pray until the heavens open, the rains fall and the seeds begin to sprout and fruit.

But when finally I changed—and thank G-d changed I have—it seemed like a gift, one of the greatest gifts I have ever received, from G-d. I not only felt and feel grateful, but downright lucky.

My nows are filled with more good times, feelings of unity, pleasant vibes in the house, happier children, a better marriage, more compatible work relationships and even less frustration when driving on Israeli roads (perhaps the real test). Plus, I get to like myself more and walk the earth without the nagging feeling that I am a menace to myself and others.

Let me be clear. I still get angry. Anger, it seems to me, is just one of those emotions that people have, whether they should or not. Certainly the ideal may be that one would never get angry, but I haven't met those folks. Or, the ones I have met are in the category of *tzaddi-kim*, the righteous ones that walk the earth and heavens.

But I don't fit in that category, nor do the people I know and have known. So, for the vast majority of us, anger is a part of life, even though I believe, as our Sages teach, that anger is akin to idol worship, that it is a denial of G-d's providence, omnipotence and omniscience.

But overcoming that denial, or rather coming to see and accept G-d's hand in every aspect of life, is another of those things, like overcoming anger, that for most of us takes a life time, if it ever happens at all, if we're ever lucky enough.

Thus, anger remains.

The difference in my life now is that I just can't tolerate it or the destruction and hurt that it causes to others. I feel it, I recognize it, I accept it, and then, when I'm lucky, I let it go, along with all the obsessive thoughts that accompany it—the accusations and condemnations, the hurt and injustice, the jealousy, the desire for revenge.

I'd like to take credit for these changes, but in truth they feel as much the result of happenstance as effort, of G-d's intervention and providence.

First, the destructiveness of my behavior in all its terror became so vivid I could not tolerate it. I not only saw this in times of anger, but also in vision and memory of angry times past, visions that I think were gifts from Above. I became tormented by all that I was capable of destroying, and had. I saw and felt the hurt and damage I was causing others with my cruel words and actions. I saw and felt it as if I were the object of my own anger. And I cringed and cried as I felt the pain and damage I was causing to those I loved most. It was as if the anger was happening all over again, but now I could see it with distance and perspective, though the feelings were as intense as if it were happening now. Not feelings of anger, but feelings of revulsion for what I was watching, for what I had done.

Second, during some recent difficult times, I have been the object of love and concern, patience and dedication by some of those at whom I had been the angriest. In the face of their kindness and of my need, I could no longer muster the anger I once had. Now, I could only feel gratitude and love and perceived in these onetime objects of my anger such angelic souls that I felt searing shame at my past actions towards them.

That they were now so loving despite the anger that I'd spent at them over the years increased their virtue even further and where once I could, in moments of blind anger, see only their negativity, now any perceived hurt

or disappointment I felt from them was balanced with my awareness of and appreciation for their goodness and kindness. And to them I ask and will continue to ask forgiveness.

I also began to more and more recognize G-d's hand in my life, and His goodness. The reality of G-d's participation in and control of the world, even in times that could be described as "bad," penetrated deeper and deeper into my psyche and soul. Thus, no matter what happened I began to see and truly believe that this, too, comes from G-d. The hurts or disappointments, the lacks and the frustrations—all come from G-d. There is no one to blame. Or if there is, it is only Him. Each obstacle, each frustration, each hurt, each fear, every childhood injury or lack comes ultimately from Him, for my benefit, as part of my life's journey—a journey tailored by Him only for me.

From this perspective I saw that anger is always wrong. It has no justification, no matter how righteous the justification feels. Acknowledging both the humanness of this emotion and its total wrongness gives me a place from which to relate to my anger. Knowing it is wrong, the mental obsessions are also wrong. There is nothing to do with my anger other than to acknowledge it and let it pass. And often, letting it pass requires that I ask, that I beg G-d to take it from me, to open my heart and my mind so that I can perceive what is taking place more compassionately, from a wider perspective, from outside myself and inside the other.

And luckily, this has taken place enough times that I am able to experience what life is like without my anger: what life in my home is like, what my relationship with my wife is like, what my relationship to myself is like, and what my relationship with G-d is like.

And, it is good. So much better than ever before. It is, without exaggeration, like a rebirth. And each moment, each day that I live without anger or even with less anger, I beg and pray that it not return. It is, in spite of its humanness, so very evil and destructive. And each day that it does not return, I thank G-d for His intervention, for the "luck" He provided and provides.

Please hear this: Even after your remorse, if you are fortunate enough to be forgiven by those you love, you will still not be able to recapture and relive all those days and nights you wasted in your anger, time that could have been spent in love and good feeling. Anger fills the irreplaceable now, disallowing the wonder that could be.

It destroys the goodness of life.

Jay Litvin was born in Chicago in 1944. He moved to Israel in 1993 to serve as medical liaison for Chabad's Children of Chernobyl program, and took a leading role in airlifting children from the areas contaminated by the Chernobyl nuclear disaster; he also founded and directed Chabad's Terror Victims program in Israel. Jay passed away in April of 2004 after a valiant four-year battle with non-Hodgkin's lymphoma, and is survived by his wife, Sharon, and their seven children. He was a frequent contributor to Chabad.org.

Reprinted with permission of The Judaism Website—Chabad.org

Lesson **5**
Sacred Space:
No Trespassing!
Defining Marriage's Boundaries

Introduction

In Judaism, a marriage is considered consummated before any conjugal act, when the bride and groom are secluded together for a few minutes following the marriage ceremony. The intimate space provided by this seclusion defines the marriage and should remain sacred and exclusive throughout the relationship. This lesson introduces practical ways to form and fortify an exclusive and powerful relationship.

The State of Exclusivity

Learning Interaction 1

Other than sexual relations, what activities should be defined as "intimate" and should remain exclusively between spouses?

_____

_____

_____

_____

_____

_____

_____

_____

_____

EXCLUSIVE

The Nature of Infidelity
Consequences

Text 1 📖

איש ואשה: זכו, שכינה ביניהן, לא זכו, אש אוכלתן.
תלמוד בבלי, סוטה יז,א

hen a husband and wife are worthy, God resides among them. If they are unworthy, a fire consumes them.

Talmud, Sotah 17a

Babylonian Talmud. A literary work of monumental proportions that draws upon the totality of the legal, spiritual, intellectual, ethical, and historical traditions of Judaism, the Babylonian Talmud was set up as a commentary to the Mishnah and was written primarily in Aramaic. The Talmud contains the teachings of the Jewish sages, mostly from the period after the destruction of the Second Temple through the fifth century C.E. The Babylonian Talmud has served as the primary vehicle for the education of countless Jews over the centuries; it is the entry point for all subsequent legal, ethical, and theological Jewish scholarship.

Question for Discussion

If an act of infidelity always remains a secret, will it be harmful to a marriage?

Prevalence

Text 2

Naomi Schaefer Riley. Affiliate scholar at the Institute for American Values and former *Wall Street Journal* editor and writer, her writing focuses on higher education, religion, philanthropy, and culture. She is the author of *God on the Quad* and *The Faculty Lounges: And Other Reasons Why You Won't Get the College Education You Pay For*.

In 2006, about 19% of married men and 13% of married women under the age of 30 said that they had been unfaithful to their spouse. . . . Between 1991 and 2006, the numbers of unfaithful wives under 30 increased by 20% and husbands by a whopping 45%. These numbers come from a study conducted by David Atkins of the University of Washington Center for the Study of Health and Risk Behaviors. . . .

The rise in infidelity among this cohort has caught some marriage experts off-guard. David Popenoe of the Marriage Project, at Rutgers University, immediately noted this oddity: Although our culture may have gotten more sexually permissive over the past 50 years, "the attitudes against adultery have gotten firmer over time." He cites one survey showing that more than 90% of the population believes that cheating on one's spouse is always wrong.

Naomi Schaefer Riley, "The Young and the Restless: Why Infidelity Is Rising Among 20-Somethings," *The Wall Street Journal*, November 28, 2008

Learning Interaction 2

What are some of the possible reasons for the recent increase in infidelity?

Phenomenon	Does this phenomenon impact the infidelity rate? (circle one)	How this contributes to infidelity
Rising age of marriage	Very Significantly Significantly Somewhat Not at all	
Onset of the Communication Age	Very Significantly Significantly Somewhat Not at all	
More women in the workplace	Very Significantly Significantly Somewhat Not at all	
Secularization of society	Very Significantly Significantly Somewhat Not at all	
Marriage is perceived less as a religious institution	Very Significantly Significantly Somewhat Not at all	
Other: _____ _____	Very Significantly Significantly Somewhat	

Causes

Learning Interaction 3

What are some of the significant factors that cause people to be unfaithful in marriage?

Factor	How significant is this factor? (circle one)
Emotional dissatisfaction in marriage	Very Significant Somewhat Significant Not at all Significant
Sexual dissatisfaction in marriage	Very Significant Somewhat Significant Not at all Significant
Human nature to always seek something more or different	Very Significant Somewhat Significant Not at all Significant
Circumstance (i.e., the opportunity arose)	Very Significant Somewhat Significant Not at all Significant
Selfishness	Very Significant Somewhat Significant Not at all Significant
Other: _____ _____	Very Significant Somewhat Significant

Text 3

"וַיִּזְעֲקוּ אֶל ה' אלקים בְּקוֹל גָּדוֹל" (נחמיה ט,ד). מאי אמור?

אמר רב ואיתימא רבי יוחנן: "בייא, בייא! היינו האי דאחרביה למקדשא, וקליה
להיכליה, וקטלינהו לכולהו צדיקי, ואגלינהו לישראל מארעהון, ועדיין מרקד בינן!
כלום יהבתיה לן אלא לקבולי ביה אגרא. לא איהו בעינן, ולא אגריה בעינן" . . .
אותיבו בתעניתא תלתא יומין ותלתא לילואתא, מסרוהו ניהליהו. נפק אתא כי גוריא
דנורא מבית קדשי הקדשים. אמר להו נביא לישראל: "היינו יצרא דעבודה זרה" . . .
אמרו: "הואיל ועת רצון הוא נבעי רחמי איצרא דעבירה". בעו רחמי ואמסר בידייהו.
אמר להו: "חזו דאי קטליתו ליה להההוא כליא עלמא".
חבשוהו תלתא יומי, ובעו ביעתא בת יומא בכל ארץ ישראל ולא אשתכח.
אמרי: "היכי נעביד? נקטליה? כליא עלמא! ניבעי רחמי אפלגא? פלגא ברקיעא לא יהבי".
כחלינהו לעיניה, ושבקוהו. ואהני דלא מיגרי ביה לאיניש בקריבתה.

תלמוד בבלי, יומא סט,ב

❝hey cried aloud to God" (Nehemiah 9:4). What was their cry?

Rav (others say Rabbi Yochanan) said, [this was their cry]: "Woe, woe! It is this [temptation for idolatry] that has caused the destruction of the Holy Temple, the burning of the sanctuary, the killing of all the righteous, and the expulsion of Israel from their land—and it is still dancing among us! You have surely given it to us so that we may earn reward through [resisting] it. We want neither it, nor the reward it potentially brings us!" . . .

They fasted three days and three nights, whereupon the temptation for idolatry was surrendered to them. It came forth from the Holy of Holies appearing as a young fiery lion. Thereupon a prophet said to Israel,

"This is the evil desire for idolatry [departing from our midst]." . . .

The sages said, "Since this is a time of grace, let us pray to [be rid of] the temptation for sexual transgression." They prayed, and this temptation, too, was handed over to them.

The temptation said to them, "Understand, if you kill me, the world will be destroyed."

They imprisoned it for three days. They then searched the entire Land of Israel for a fresh egg, but there were none.

They said, "What shall we do now? Shall we kill it? The world would then cease to exist. Shall we pray that we retain [the positive] half and destroy [the negative] half? Heaven will not grant half."

They blinded its eyes and released it. It helped inasmuch as temptation no more entices people to commit incest.

Talmud, Yoma 69b

Question for Discussion

What message is conveyed by this Talmudic passage?

Text 4 📜

הנך שבוייתא דאתאי לנהרדעא, אסקינהו לבי רב עמרם חסידא,
אשקולו דרגא מקמייהו.

בהדי דקא חלפה חדא מנייהו, נפל נהורא באיפומא, שקליה רב עמרם לדרגא . . . דלייא
לחודיה. סליק ואזיל, כי מטא לפלגא דרגא איפשח, רמא קלא: "נורא בי עמרם!"

אתו רבנן, אמרו ליה, "כסיפתינן!"

אמר להו, "מוטב תיכספו בי עמרם בעלמא הדין, ולא תיכספו מיניה לעלמא דאתי".

תלמוד בבלי, קידושין פא,א

Some captive women [were ransomed and] brought to Nehardea. They were taken to the [second story of the] house of Rav Amram the Pious, and the ladder was removed from beneath them.

As one of the women passed by [the hatch that served as the passageway between the two stories], a light shone through the hatch. Rav Amram seized a [very heavy] ladder . . . and he alone lifted it, [set it up,] and proceeded to ascend. When he had gone half way [up the ladder], he steadied his feet and bellowed in a loud voice, "A fire at Rav Amram's!"

The rabbis came [running to help extinguish the fire. Seeing that there was no fire, and understanding what Rav Amram was about to do, they] reproved him, "We are ashamed of you!"

Said he to them, "Better that you be ashamed of Amram in this world than that you be ashamed of him in the next."

Talmud, Kidushin 81a

Setting Boundaries
Yichud

Text 5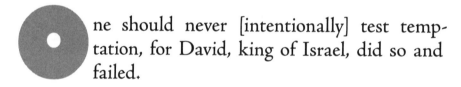

לעולם אל יביא אדם עצמו לידי נסיון, שהרי דוד מלך ישראל הביא עצמו לידי נסיון
ונכשל.

אמר לפניו: "רבונו של עולם, מפני מה אומרים, 'אלקי אברהם אלקי יצחק ואלקי
יעקב' ואין אומרים 'אלקי דוד'"?

אמר, "אינהו מינסו לי, ואת לא מינסית לי".

אמר לפניו, "רבונו של עולם, בחנני ונסני" . . .

אמר, "מינסנא לך. ועבידנא מילתא בהדך, דלדידהו לא הודעתינהו ואילו אנא קא
מודענא לך דמנסינא לך בדבר ערוה".

תלמוד בבלי, סנהדרין קז,א

One should never [intentionally] test temptation, for David, king of Israel, did so and failed.

King David said to God, "Master of the Universe! Why do we say [in prayer] 'The God of Abraham, the God of Isaac, and the God of Jacob,' but not 'the God of David'?"

"They were tested by Me, but you were not," was the response.

David replied, "Master of the Universe, test and try me." . . .

God responded, "I will test you, and even grant you a special privilege; for I did not inform the patriarchs [in advance the nature of their trial], yet, I inform you that I will test you in a matter of a forbidden sexual relationship."

Talmud, Sanhedrin 107a

Question for Discussion

What kind of rule or guideline would inhibit people from being unfaithful?

Question for Discussion

What is the logic behind the prohibition of *yichud*?

Text 6

אין לך דבר בכל התורה כולה שהוא קשה לרוב העם לפרוש אלא מן העריות והביאות
האסורות. אמרו חכמים: בשעה שנצטוו ישראל על העריות בכו וקבלו מצוה זו
בתרעומות ובכיה . . .

ואמרו חכמים: גזל ועריות, נפשו של אדם מתאוה להן ומחמדתן, ואין אתה מוצא קהל
בכל זמן וזמן שאין בהן פרוצין בעריות וביאות אסורות . . .

לפיכך ראוי לו לאדם לכוף יצרו בדבר זה, ולהרגיל עצמו בקדושה יתירה ובמחשבה
טהורה ובדעה נכונה כדי להנצל מהן.

ויזהר מן הייחוד שהוא הגורם הגדול.

משנה תורה, הלכות איסורי ביאה כב,יח–כ

There is no Torah prohibition that is more difficult for the majority of people to abstain from than sexual misconduct. Our sages said: When the Jews were commanded regarding forbidden sexual relations, they wept and received this mitzvah with grumbling and tears. . . .

Our sages said: A person desires and craves . . . forbidden sexual relations. You will never find a community

Rabbi Moshe ben Maimon (1135–1204). Better known as Maimonides or by the acronym Rambam; born in Cordoba, Spain. After the conquest of Cordoba by the Almohads, he fled Spain and eventually settled in Cairo, Egypt. There, he became the leader of the Jewish community and served as court physician to the vizier of Egypt. His rulings on Jewish law are considered integral to the formation of halachic consensus. He is most noted for authoring the *Mishneh Torah,* an encyclopedic arrangement of Jewish law, and for his philosophical work, *Guide for the Perplexed.*

that does not have promiscuous people who engage in sexual misconduct. . . .

Therefore, it is proper for people to master their desires and train themselves to behave in an exceedingly holy manner, to think pure thoughts, and cultivate proper character traits in order to guard against sexual impropriety.

And one should be careful with regard to *yichud*, for it is the greatest trigger.

Maimonides, *Mishneh Torah*, Laws of Prohibited Relations 22:18–20

Emotional Infidelity

Text 7

When we think "affair," we think sex. Sex outside marriage can be a knife through a spouse's heart. But an emotional affair can be just as dangerous to a marriage, and often a more complicated situation to remedy. *When a spouse places his or her primary emotional needs in the hands of someone outside the marriage, it breaks the bond of marriage just as adultery does. . . .*

You have only so much energy. If you're spending it with coworkers . . . then getting home and feeling too tired to spend any more on your spouse, that's emotional infidelity. You're effectively relocating vital marital energy into the hands of others. Forget about where it might end up. Even if you never touch this other person, you have still used that person to relate to, and in doing so, you relate away from your spouse. . . .

The first step in developing a happy marriage is to close our peripheral vision to others so that we can be fully focused on our mate. . . .

Countless people have told me that getting involved with members of the opposite sex isn't a problem for them because it would never lead to adultery. . . . Sex is far from the only problem. You will simply be chipping away at your marriage every time you get that ping of excitement from an emotionally stimulating moment with someone of the opposite sex. It's dangerous to your marriage, and not because it may lead to sex. Rather, it drains your marriage of the immense energy it needs to grow: the energy to flirt with each other, to be emotionally stimulated by a different point of view, to share the excitement with someone who wants to know who you are. When you place your emotional energies elsewhere, without even realizing it, you don't offer your spouse the opportunity to provide you with that same ping of excitement you are looking for elsewhere.

M. Gary Neuman, *Emotional Infidelity* [New York: Crown, 2001], pp. 26–35

M. Gary Neuman is a licensed psychotherapist, ordained rabbi, and founder of the Sandcastles Program, a nationwide divorce therapy program for children. He is a frequent guest on national TV and radio and is the *New York Times* bestselling author of *The Truth About Cheating, Emotional Infidelity,* and *Helping Your Kids Cope with Divorce the Sandcastles Way.* He lives in Miami with his wife and five children.

Text 8

Rabbi Yosef Rosen, "the Rogatchover Ga'on" (1858–1936), he was one of the prominent Talmudic scholars of the early 20th century. Born in Rogatchov, Belarus, to a chasidic family, his unusual capabilities were recognized at a young age. At thirteen he was brought to Slutsk to study with Rabbi Yosef Ber Soloveitchik. He remained there for a full year, studying primarily with the rabbi's son, the legendary Chaim Soloveitchik. After a period in Warsaw, the home city of his wife, he assumed the rabbinate of the chasidic community in Dvinsk. His works, titled *Tsafenat Pane'ach*, are famed for both their depth and difficulty.

לענין יחוד הוא גם כן יש בו ב׳ גדרי איסורים: אחד משום דהוה גדר קריבה, והב׳ משום חשש תקלה.

צפנת פענח, הלכות איסורי ביאה כא,ד

There are two reasons for the prohibition of *yichud*. Firstly, it constitutes a form of intimacy. Secondly, it can potentially lead to immoral behavior.

Rabbi Yosef Rosen, Tsafenat Pane'ach, Hilchot Isurei Bi'ah 21:4

Text 9

Everybody needs a friend at work. But many people go beyond friendship to find an "office spouse"—a worker of the opposite sex who shares not only office gossip and job woes, but confidences, loyalties and a close emotional bond. . . .

Nearly two-thirds of workers have, or have had, a "work spouse"—a close co-worker of the opposite sex who shares confidences, loyalties and experiences, according to a survey last July of 640 white-collar workers. Beyond talking about the office, more than half of these pairs discuss health issues or at-home problems, and 35% even talk about their sex lives, says the survey by Captivate Network, a digital-programming company.

The couples I interviewed say having a work husband or work wife can make going to the office a lot more fun. Sharing frustrations and stress over office politics and problems with bosses or co-workers eases stress.

But such relationships can easily cross the line into an emotional affair.

Sue Shellenbarger, "Do You Have a 'Work Spouse'?"
The Wall Street Journal, February 8, 2011

Sue Shellenbarger. Columnist for *The Wall Street Journal*, she created and writes the "Work & Family" column that covers the growing conflict between work and family and its implications for the workplace and society. Her column has received seven major national awards. Her most recent book, *The Breaking Point*, is about midlife crisis in women.

The Spirit of *Yichud*

Optional Section

Text 10 ▌

Rabbi Shalom Dovber Schneersohn, "the Rebbe Rashab" (1860–1920). A Chasidic rebbe and 5th leader of the Chabad movement, he is the author of many volumes of chasidic discourses, renowned for their encyclopedic method of expounding upon kabbalistic concepts. He established the Lubavitch network of *yeshivot* called Tomchei Temimim. Born in Lubavitch, he became rebbe at the age of 21, upon the passing of his father, the Rebbe Maharash. During World War I, he fled to Rostov on the Don, Russia, where he is buried.

ישנם בני אדם אשר רחוקים המה מאיזה דבר רע בפועל חס ושלום, אבל לבם מושך אותם לראות ולהביט, וההבטה היא כמו בקר רוח ואינו מרגיש בעצמו בעת מעשה איזה התפעלות . . . וההבטה, עם היותה בקר רוח לכאורה, הנה היא עושה רושם וחקיקה גדולה בנפש.

קונטרס העבודה, פרק ב

There are those who are above actually doing anything improper, God forbid, yet their heart draws them to gaze [at that which is forbidden]. The gaze is cold; the person does not feel any excitement.... Though there is no noticeable excitement, that which is seen has a deep effect and leaves an imprint on the person's soul.

Rabbi Shalom Dovber Schneersohn, *Kuntres Ha'avodah* 2

End of Optional Section

Stolen Waters

Text 11a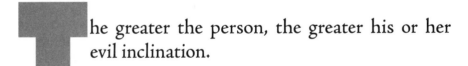

לעתיד לבא, מביאו הקדוש ברוך הוא ליצר הרע ושוחטו בפני הצדיקים ובפני הרשעים.
צדיקים נדמה להם כהר גבוה, ורשעים נדמה להם כחוט השערה.
תלמוד בבלי, סוכה נב,א

In the future, God will slay the evil inclination in the presence of the righteous and the wicked. To the righteous, it will have the appearance of a towering mountain, and to the wicked, it will have the appearance of a hairsbreadth.

Talmud, Sukah 52a

Text 11b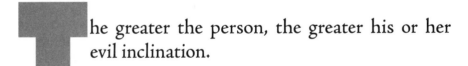

כל הגדול מחבירו יצרו גדול הימנו.
תלמוד בבלי, שם

The greater the person, the greater his or her evil inclination.

Talmud, ibid.

Question for Discussion

These Talmudic passages imply that temptation is greater for the righteous than the non-righteous. Why is this?

Text 12 📜

המתבונן בתאות האדם בעולם הזה יראה ברור כי כל תאותו הוא לדבר שאין בידו. וכל שהוא רחוק ונעול ממנו גברה תאותו יותר עליו. וכמאמרם בחזרת הממון, "מי שיש לו מנה מבקש מאתים".

ורואים אנחנו הרבה פעמים בעל יפת מראה עובר עבירה עם מכוערה, מי שיש לו מאכל טוב ויפה חומד למאכל גס. וכל אלו משום דכל דבר שישנו בידו וברשותו לא נחשב בעיניו, וכל תאותו רק למה שאין בידו. וזה כלל גדול בתאות עולם הזה. וכבר כללן הכתוב במליצתו "מים גנובים ימתקו ולחם סתרים ינעם" (משלי ט,יז). דכיון שהם גנובים ואין בידו לאוכלם ולשתותם בפני כל כי אם במחבא, נעמים לחכו . . . ומאותו טעם, דבר עבירה, כיון שאסורה על האדם ולאו הוא כמו בהיתר, משום הכי נפשו של אדם מחמדתן.

וחמדה זו הוא לפי ערך האדם ביראת חטא: כל שהוא גדול ביראת חטא יצרו ותאותו גדולה יותר, דכיון שהיא נעולה וגדורה טפי ולאו ברשותו לעשותה ולמלאות תאותו, נפשו מחמדתה יותר.

מבשרי אחזה, נא

There's a general rule concerning material desires: Human beings desire that which they do not have. The more distant and elusive an enticement, the more powerful the temptation to attain it. As our sages say concerning the pursuit of money: "One who has one hundred desires two hundred."

We often see a handsome man committing a sin with an unattractive woman, or someone who has tasty and healthful foods desiring simple and unwholesome foods. This is because a person considers insignificant that which he or she already has, and desires that which is out of reach.

The Scriptures allegorically allude to this idea: "Stolen waters are sweet, and hidden bread is pleasant" (Proverbs

9:17). Because they are stolen, they cannot be eaten in public, only in hiding, and therefore they are pleasant to the palate.... It is for this reason that the temptation for the forbidden is so powerful—the very fact that it is forbidden makes it so desirable.

Thus, the degree to which one is tempted by the forbidden directly corresponds to the person's piety. One who is more pious will have more powerful lusts and desires, inasmuch as the forbidden is very much beyond his or her reach.

Rabbi Yechezkel Rotner, *Mibesari Echezeh* 51

Rabbi Yechezkel Rotner (19th century) was a rabbi in Mogilev, today in Belarus, and was well known for his wealth and philanthropy as well as his scholarship. Among his works are *Responsa Yevaser Tov* (Vilna, 1868) and *Responsa Mibesari Echezeh* (1874).

מי שיש לו מנה מבקש מאתים

Text 13 📜

אמר להו רב חסדא לבנתיה . . . "נקיט מרגניתא בחדא ידיה, וכורא בחדא ידיה. מרגניתא אחוי להו, וכורא לא אחוי להו עד דמיצטערן, והדר אחוי להו."

תלמוד בבלי, שבת קמ,ב

Rav Chisda advised his daughters. . . . "[In the course of intimacy, when your husband wishes to] hold the pearl in one hand and the kiln in the other hand, you should offer the pearl, but the kiln you should not offer until he is tormented. Only then shall you offer it to him."

Talmud, Shabbat 140b

Text 14 📜

ואחרי שהאדם בטבעו משליך כל הדברים שברשותו אחרי גיוו וכאין נחשבו לו, רק שוטף כסוס אחרי הדברים שאינם ברשותו, הרי האדם בסכנה עצומה בעולם הזה. כי ההיתר הוא בידו באין מפריע, והאיסור גדור ונעול ממנו מפני הצווי שנצטוה שלא לעשותו, ויהיה תמיד לבו רודפו אחרי האיסור, ולא בנקל יהיה לבן אדם לכבוש תאותו. על כן יעצו עצת חכם אשר כל אדם לא יגמור כל תאותו אף בדברים המותרים שהן בידו, רק יניח קצת מהן. וכיון שהוא כובש הלב ומגדיר בעד קצת התאוה, אז היא מתאבקת וטרודה בזה ואין לה פנאי לרדוף אחרי האיסור . . .

ועצה זו שמעינן מדברי רב חסדא לבנתיה, שיעץ להם שלא יניחו לגמור כל תאותן בהן. כי אחרי שיהיה בידן לגמור בהן כל תאותן ככל חפצן, שוב פסק מהן המים גנובים, היינו דברים שאין ברשותן, ויהיה לבן רודפן לחבק חיק זרות שהם מים גנובים.

מבשרי אחזה, נא

Since people are naturally uninterested in things that they have, and instead chase after things they do not and cannot have, this leaves them in a dangerous predicament. The permissible they have, while the forbidden is unattainable. This will cause them to constantly pursue the forbidden, and it will be very difficult for a person to control these desires.

Therefore it is advisable not to fulfill all our desires, though they are permitted and available; rather, we should leave some desires unfulfilled. We will then be consumed by these permitted desires, because they are "off limits," and there will be no energy or headspace to focus on the forbidden. . . .

This advice we derive from Rav Chisda's counsel to his daughters, that they not allow their husbands to fulfill all of their desires. For if their husbands were to freely get all that they wish, there would be no "stolen waters" within the marriage, and their passions might tempt them to find the "stolen waters" in the embrace of others' bosoms.

Rabbi Yechezkel Rotner, *Mibsari Echezeh* 51

Expanding Your Marriage

Text 15a

דּוֹדִי לִי וַאֲנִי לוֹ.

שיר השירים ב,טז

My beloved is mine, and I am his.

Song of Songs 2:16

Text 15b

Rabbi Shlomo Yitschaki (1040–1105). Better known by the acronym Rashi. Rabbi and famed author of comprehensive commentaries on the Talmud and Bible. Born in Troyes, France, Rashi studied in the famed *yeshivot* of Mainz and Worms. His commentaries, which focus on the simple understanding of the text, are considered the most fundamental of all commentaries. Since their initial printings, the commentaries have appeared in virtually every edition of the Talmud and Bible. Many of the famed authors of the *Tosafot* are among Rashi's descendants.

"דודי לי"—הוא כל צרכיו תבע ממני, ולא צוה אלא לי עשו פסח, קדשו בכורות, עשו משכן, הקריבו עולות, ולא תבע מאומה אחרת. "ואני לו"—כל צרכי תבעתי ממנו, ולא מאלהים אחרים.

רש"י, שם

My beloved is mine—He asks me to provide all His needs. Only to me did He instruct to bring a Paschal offering, consecrate the firstborn, construct a Tabernacle, and offer burnt sacrifices. He did not ask these things of any other nation.

And I am his—All my needs I asked only Him to provide, not other gods.

Rashi, ad loc.

Key Points

1. Infidelity undermines the sanctity of marriage and, practically speaking, has devastating consequences for a relationship.

2. The scourge of extramarital affairs strikes many people who are morally opposed to infidelity.

3. Improving one's marital relationship decreases the chance of infidelity, but is not a foolproof guarantee. This is because every human being, even the pious and those deeply in love with their spouses, can be tempted to sexually stray.

4. Seclusion with a member of the opposite gender removes a very important barrier—shame—that holds us back from acting immorally. Avoiding seclusion also helps ensure that feelings of closeness are not generated.

5. A spouse who places his or her primary emotional needs in the hands of someone outside the marriage is breaking the bond of marriage and is not fully focused on his or her mate. The laws of *yichud* help one avoid the trap of "emotional affairs."

6. The concept of "family purity" introduces a degree of the sweetness of "stolen waters" to a marriage, thus mitigating one of the factors that causes infidelity.

7. We can improve our marital relationships by expanding the exclusivity of our marriages to a variety of activities and arenas.

Additional Readings

Secret #1
(Selected Excerpts)

by **M. Gary Neuman**

Commitment is the glue of marriage. Insulate and protect your marriage against emotional infidelity by avoiding friendships with members of the opposite sex.

All of us know that adultery—sex outside the marriage—is one of the gravest blows to a marriage as well as a painful rejection for one partner. But you don't have to have *sex* with anyone else to be unfaithful. *Emotional infidelity* is just as—and at times even more—destructive to your marriage. Couples I counsel are absolutely outraged when I tell them that they could well be committing emotional adultery when they flirt with coworkers, send around funny e-mails to colleagues, or hang out with members of the opposite sex at gatherings. But they are, and so probably are you.

You're not going to want to hear this, but stopping this kind of relationship is the single most important thing you can do for your marriage. *It's not about where it may lead. It's about where it has already gone,* far from your focus on your marriage. You may be incensed by what I have to say. You may feel uncomfortable when you hear how I define *relationships* with members of the opposite sex. That's fine. My purpose here is to challenge you to take a close, and almost certainly uncomfortable, look at what you're doing and why, and to help you see how it's hurting your marriage

When you find yourself getting irritated with what I have to say, consider: Why does it bother you? Why are you resisting the idea? Why not see if I'm right by making some changes? What is it that you're trying to protect by maintaining the kind of relationships you're

presently involved in? If these relationships aren't as "damaging" as I say, because you say you don't find them that important and they aren't going to lead anywhere, then prove it to yourself by letting go of them. If they don't mean that much to you, why the irritation when I ask you to cut back on these friendships? Remember what it is you've always wanted from your marriage, and start considering the large, determined commitment that is absolutely necessary to creating a happy marriage. . . .

***

Leon was the first person in my counseling practice to drive home a message often lost in our collective marital minds. Leon had been married for nine years. He and his wife, Maribel, had two handsome sons, ages six and four, a waterfront home, and a golden retriever. Life was going really well until Leon fell in love with another woman. When Leon and Maribel came to see me to see if they could survive this crisis, they both cried in disbelief that this could happen to them. Oddly, Leon had never met the "other woman." In fact, he'd never ever heard this woman's voice. But he knew her e-mail address and had been in private chat rooms with her every night for months.

Leon was distraught and perplexed as he told me his story. He didn't know how or when it happened, but this woman now held the key to his heart. After all, his cyber pal truly understood him. They thought so much alike. She knew the right things to say, or rather write. She had great advice on how to help him reduce his stress at work and seemed so kind and warm. She often inquired about Maribel and the kids and always reminded him that his wife and family came first before her. But Leon's wife gradually took a back seat to his cyber fantasy woman. All of Leon's emotional energy went into his e-mails to this woman.

Leon had never thought it would come to this. Because this other woman lived in a different country, there was no chance of foul play, he rationalized. His marital vows would remain intact as long as he never strayed physically. But recently Leon and the woman had sent each other their photographs. Leon had the envelope at work and had yet to open it, knowing that seeing his cyber love might irreparably damage his marriage.

***

You Don't Have to Have Sex to Cheat on Your Marriage

When we think "affair," we think sex. Sex outside the marriage can be a knife through a spouse's heart. But an emotional affair can be just as dangerous to a marriage, and often a more complicated situation to remedy. *When a spouse places his or her primary emotional needs in the hands of someone outside the marriage, it breaks the bond of marriage just as adultery does.*

The moment Leon fell in love with this mystery woman, he fell out of love with his wife. Instead of focusing on overcoming the challenges in his marriage, he found excitement in relating to another woman. As he shared his struggles, laughter, fears, and joy with his cyber mate, he drained his marriage of the emotional effervescence and renewal it needed to thrive. He would return home after work and avoid discussing his day with Maribel, knowing he'd have to repeat it all later at the keyboard. With two sons around, it was easy not to find private time with his wife. When Leon and Maribel did talk, it was either about disciplining the boys or money, two unavoidable and unromantic issues. Leon's emotional affair placed his marriage on the brink of destruction. Now that Leon had found fulfillment through his nightly cyber chats, which were devoid of the dull, day-to-day stuff of running a household, he'd stopped making any effort to relate to Maribel. Naturally, she felt rejected.

Leon might sound like an extreme situation. True, most of us won't fall in love in cyber space, yet we find it okay to share a different kind of space with friends of the opposite sex. We discuss our problems, air out our issues, and settle disagreements with our business colleagues. We chat with our friends and neighbors. What's the harm in a man having a casual friendship with a woman when either is married? Surely, every friendship doesn't lead to an affair. Yet we forget the emotional harm of relating to someone outside the marriage when that same energy can be used to relate to our own spouse. Marriage is about relating to a member of the opposite sex with an intimacy felt with no other.

Even if Leon never "fell in love" with his cyber pal, his relationship with this other woman was still whittling away at his marriage. He was closing the door on his ability to relate to his wife in those areas that he chose to share with another.

How Do You Know If You're Being Unfaithful?

Consider your own personal relationships:

• When you hear a funny joke or good piece of gossip, do you first tell other colleagues? By the time you get home, have you chewed it all over so much at the office that you don't feel like telling that joke again to your spouse?

• Do you discuss all of your work problems (or issues involving volunteer work or other important things you are involved in) so thoroughly with colleagues that you're all talked out by the time you return home? Do you feel like it would take too long to review and explain the entire issue from scratch to your spouse?

• Do you go out alone to lunch or after work for drinks with members of the opposite sex?

• Do you enjoy harmless (by your definition) flirtation with someone of the opposite sex at a cocktail party?

• Do you believe that getting emotionally excited by flirting with someone of the opposite sex is helpful to your marriage? Do you think it helps educate you as to what you need more of from your spouse? Do you tell yourself that the juice you get from flirting brings more vitality to your marriage?

• Do you spend as long buying the "right gift" for a colleague of the opposite sex as you do for your own spouse?

• Do you ride in a car sharing pleasant, personal conversation alone with a member of the opposite sex on the way to meetings or other work-related events?

• Do you share intimate issues about yourself or marriage with a member of the opposite sex?

If you're doing any of these things, you're being emotionally unfaithful to your spouse. You have only so much energy. If you're spending it with coworkers or outside the home and then getting home and feeling too tired to spend any more on your spouse, that's emotional infidelity. You're effectively relocating vital marital energy into the hands of others. Forget about where it might end up. Even if you never touch this other person, you have still used that person to relate to, and in doing so, you relate away from your spouse.

You may be shaking your head and disagreeing. But I've spent years helping couples pool their energies toward each other, and it has changed their marriage immediately. Stop all of these outside relationships and bring all your emotional and sexual energy home to *your* spouse, and you, too, will change your marriage immediately. . . .

Fidelity Facts

Although 98 percent of Americans believe it's wrong to have an affair,[1] infidelity looms large in our marital world. Statistics vary greatly as to how widespread it is. Research estimates of how many husbands and wives are unfaithful range from 15 to 70 percent.[2] In fact, one poll showed that over half would not consider virtual sex as having an affair.[3] Another study cited infidelity as the number one reason (31 percent) for divorce.[4] When infidelity strikes, there is a 65 percent chance that the marriage will end in divorce.[5] As psychiatrist Frank Pittman believes, "There may be as many acts of

infidelity in our society as there are traffic accidents."[6] Dr. Pittman claims that after being involved in seven thousand divorce cases in thirty-nine years, "I've seen only five established first marriages ending in divorce without somebody being unfaithful. Every year I think I've seen the sixth, but I wait, and sure enough the other man or woman surfaces even though they deny and deny and deny."[7] Regardless of any statistic, it is clear that infidelity is a common fear in any marriage. We should never minimize its potential or its danger. . . .

Isolation Makes Sense

I recognize that some may find my idea of marital isolation archaic and unrealistic. Yet we are comfortable applying the same logic to many other areas in life. If we were to start a business, for example, we'd understand the need to focus serious attention on it. If we were to start two businesses simultaneously, others would count the minutes until we filed for bankruptcy. If we started a family, we'd feel obligated to focus our attention on the child. We wouldn't dream of spending large amounts of time alone with another child. We'd know it would be wrong to limit time with our own kid in favor of another kid who seemed "neater" than our own. As a parent, you'd understand your obligation to find the parts of your child you love and to learn to focus more on those wonderful points. You'd want to find activities that brought out the best in your child and yourself.

Marriage needs the same commitment to developing a loving and satisfying relationship. We can't divide ourselves in many directions without losing the intensity in our marriage. Our energy is already split between our jobs, our kids, and our marriage. The only way to keep a marriage strong is to put it first and foremost always. Just because we live in an ever-changing, "enlightened" world doesn't mean we should eliminate healthy marital concepts because they sound archaic.

If you find yourself quick to dismiss my recommendation because it's "ridiculous," "unrealistic," or any other

---

[1] University of Chicago survey, as quoted by Jabeen Bhatti in "Infidelity Still Scorned: Cheating Goes On But Remains Frowned Upon"; www.infidelity.com/channels/infidelity.html.

[2] Knox, 1984: 50% of men and 20–40% of women. Michael et al.: 1994, 25% of men and 15% of women. Maggie Scarf, *Intimate Partners* (New York: Alfred Knopf, 1987): 70% of married women.

[3] CTV/Agnus Reid Group Poll, September 14, 1997.

[4] *The Guardian*, May 2, 1998: Marriage, Cohabitation and Divorce Statistics.

[5] Kerby Anderson, www.probe.org/docs/adultery.html.

[6] Frank Pittman, *Private Lies: Infidelity and the Betrayal of Intimacy* (New York: Norton, 1989).

[7] "Immunized Against Infidelity," *Chicago Tribune*, August 8, 1998.

pejorative, ask yourself whether you're being defensive. Challenge yourself to pinpoint the reasons you find my advice so irritating. Could you be avoiding a deeper commitment to your spouse and looking for reasons to excuse it? . . .

Affairs Happen in Good Marriages, Too

Many people think that if you have a good marriage, you don't have to worry about having an affair. That's what Leon thought too. Do you believe that affairs happen only to people who've been suffering in a bad marriage for some time? Do you believe that as long as the couple is communicating and working together, they don't need to take these precautions? You're mistaken. Of course, it's more likely for someone to have an affair in the midst of a troubled marriage than in the midst of marital bliss. But I've seen too many divorcing couples for whom an "innocent" emotional affair permanently undermined what both people thought was a good marriage.

Too many people divorce today because they don't understand the concept of commitment. They saw their spouse as kind of a glorified friend. They didn't focus on the responsibility that comes with marrying the person who's supposed to become your soulmate. You don't fight the heavyweight champion of the world on two hours of training a day, and you don't look for a deep, intense love that makes you feel complete in your spousal relationship without a world of commitment.

The "Love Nuptial"

All of us know the cliché: Men seem to be born with a biological fear of commitment. Many men (and women) can barely stand the idea of lifelong sexual commitment, let alone the emotional one I've outlined. The explosive divorce rate has created many marital cynics, even though research shows that relationships between unmarried people are less happy and more prone to dissolution.[8] Skeptical from the start, too many people wonder where their relationship will end up and whether love will last. With prenups and postnups, the

message about love is clear: Let's give it a shot. Maybe it'll work, maybe not. Is that all love deserves? How sad that people may never experience marital happiness because of this laissez-faire attitude, because their minds have forgotten how to dream and their hearts have forgotten how to love.

Prenuptial agreements are the height of cynicism. Although I clearly understand the legal concept, their purpose is at odds with committing oneself to marriage. The legal document signed by both parties presupposes that this union may get busted. The legal recognition that love may not last has to affect a couple, even if unconsciously. This recognition has to play a role in undermining the commitment made between these two lovers. There has to be some worry, some distance that is created by the notion that we've already signed something that will make it easier and cleaner to get divorced.

In their 1983 study of six thousand American couples (the most recent study on the subject I could find), sociologists Blumstein and Schwartz found that couples who signed prenuptial agreements felt a lack of trust in their union that they believed was harmful to their marriage.[9] Worse yet, the prenuptial suggests an attitude antithetical to marriage—that after marriage we can somehow, if even just financially, revert to the same beings we were before marriage. Marriage is about immediate and effective change through the growth of giving your whole self to another and receiving the same in return. Everything must change: our emotional, physical, and financial selves must service a new kingdom, the one of marital union. If we could ever go back to the way we were before marriage, then we never knew the genuine meaning of marriage.

I have the engaged couples I counsel sign a new kind of prenup, the "Love Nuptial": a written promise (although not meant to be legally binding) that states a lifelong responsibility to each other, that details an agreement to try new and different things if either person feels love isn't working and to seek objective help from counselors or clergy whenever one spouse requests it. If either party isn't comfortable signing the Love Nuptial, it indicates that he or she needs more time and understanding

---

[8] Susan McRae, Oxford Brookes University, research on 300 women.

[9] Blumstein, P. W., and Schwartz, P. (New York: Morrow, 1983).

about love before getting married. I also use this agreement as a postnuptial for those who are already married.

When you make the choice to truly commit to each other, you face a huge obstacle: the world around you doesn't understand commitment. They don't know that you really plan to live the rest of your life with your spouse. No, you don't want to do it in pain and misery. But it can be wonderful only if you learn to be there through thick and thin. When you know that you can be at your very lowest and your spouse will put loving arms around you and pledge undying love, you're married forever. Ironically, marriages have the potential to grow the most in times of need and difficulty. When we offer and receive love in times of need, it develops an incredible trust and appreciation for our spouse. If we can just banish the urge to find this kind of love outside our spousal relationship, we'll be forced to put incredible effort into the greatest thing we have going: our marriage. If you feel you are missing that "connection" with your spouse, choose to find the way to create a new bond with your spouse instead of looking to an opposite sex friend to fulfill you.

Countless people have told me that getting involved with members of the opposite sex isn't a problem for them because it would never lead to adultery. They've even believed that a little flirtatiousness now and then is healthy, reminding us that we're still attractive to the world at large. Sex is far from the only problem. You will simply be chipping away at your marriage every time you get that ping of excitement from an emotionally stimulating moment with someone of the opposite sex. It's dangerous to your marriage, and not because it may lead to sex. Rather, it drains your marriage of the immense energy it needs to grow: the energy to flirt with each other, to be emotionally stimulated by a different point of view, to share the excitement with someone who wants to know who you are. When you place your emotional energies elsewhere, without even realizing it, you don't offer your spouse the opportunity to provide you with that same ping of excitement you are looking for elsewhere.

***

One couple I counseled, Mark and Karen, were both vehemently opposed to this concept. They had attended a seminar of mine and sat there with arms folded, clearly disagreeing with my position. Mark had an assistant who had been his "right-hand woman" for over twelve years, two years longer than he had known his own wife. His wife, Karen, had opened an e-business with a partner the year she and Mark were married. They were so invested in these other relationships from an emotional and business standpoint that they found the idea that these involvements could be draining their marriage of energy quite preposterous. Mark used to say he was thankful for two days: the day he met Karen and the day he met his assistant. Neither spouse had ever had sex outside of the marriage, and they both felt that these other relationships had only positive effects on their life.

Two years after the seminar, Mark made an appointment to see me and related the following story. He'd fallen on hard business times and ended up in bankruptcy, thus ending his business relationship with his assistant, although they remained friends. "I found another business I wanted to start developing, and I wanted to share it with Karen," he told me. "After all, I had no one to really talk to about it, since my assistant was no longer with me. But Karen was never home, and when she was, she was too involved in business with her partner to focus on what I was saying."

Mark explained that especially after his bankruptcy, his wife's focus on her business became even more important to both of them. "It was terrible. I felt so alone, and when I told Karen that we needed to share more, she had the attitude of like, 'Excuse me? I'm really busy here.' It wasn't long before I began to resent the time she spent talking to her partner when she had such little time to talk to me. And even when I'd ask her to just tell me what was going on with her business, she'd reply that she was tired of it, that she wanted to veg out from it all when she got home. She even once told me if I wanted to hear so much about her day, I should call her partner, because she'd already told him."

Mark had never understood how much time and energy he and Karen were funneling away from each other. Only after life changed and he lost his assistant did he notice that he had lost the most important partner of all. He never thought Karen was having an affair with her partner—far from it. He felt secure that this man wasn't her "physical type." But every night Mark began to notice a certain enthusiasm in Karen whenever she spoke to her partner on the phone, a certain chuckle that seemed to grace every conversation, an excitement about their exchange of ideas, and even stress that Mark quickly began to envy. He didn't have, and realized he had never had, that kind of relationship with Karen, the ease of conversation, the laughter, and the enthusiasm.

When Mark articulated his dismay over Karen's relationship with her partner, she reminded him that he'd done the same since the beginning of their marriage with his own assistant and she'd never complained. She reminded him of his running joke for years of how each of their respective friends kept their marriage together, because these friends offered something that neither of them had for each other in their marriage. He couldn't argue with her points. He knew she was doing nothing wrong according to their marital belief system.

Two years earlier, the idea of limiting those outside relationships had sounded impossible to both Mark and Karen. They even felt that their respective businesses needed the close personal relationships they had each developed with a member of the opposite sex to survive. To have limited those relationships would have taken a supreme commitment and could potentially have destroyed their businesses. But now, even though Mark was plenty busy with the creation of his new business, he had enormous energy and desire to connect with Karen emotionally, but his wife had little interest or energy.

"I had been running from the truth," he told me. "All those years my assistant was as much my confidant as my wife. And our marriage worked. It seemed pretty good. But it doesn't look so good anymore, and I can't help but wonder how much better our marriage could have been if we'd put all that energy into each other. Basically, we found in others what we couldn't find in each other instead of finding a way to have that 'magic' in our own marriage." The relationship deteriorated quickly as Mark resented his wife's outside relationship more and more and she only responded with disinterest whenever he broached the subject. They were on the brink of marital disaster, and it had absolutely nothing

to do with sex. Neither of them was remotely sexually attracted to these other friends. Their marriage was being torn apart because of emotional infidelity.

***

Be cautious not to discount my theory about emotional infidelity. You may find multiple reasons to show how it doesn't apply to you: "I'm not going to have sex." "My spouse and I do talk as much as other couples." "My spouse really isn't interested in that part of my life, so there's no harm in sharing it with someone else." "It's good for my spouse to see that others find me attractive." "I repeat all of my conversations to my spouse." But consider one thing: Why are you searching for a way around this concept? If these other relationships really mean so little to you that they aren't hurting your marriage and would never lead to sex, why resist the idea that you should stop them and avoid them for the future? Perhaps you should realize that you're getting more from these opposite-sex relationships than you're willing to admit and thus have reason to end them.

Refocus on the one you married and how you can get whatever it is you're getting from these other relationships from your own marriage. Find outside relationships with members of the same sex and keep the "chemistry" between you and your spouse.

Emotional Infidelity at the Office

Since men and women work side by side, and with modern technology like the Internet, it has never been easier to meet and bond with others. I'm not asking you to assume a curled-up, catatonic position in the corner of a room every time a member of the opposite sex enters. We are often required not only to spend time with members of the opposite sex but to be sensitive to them and to get to know them. Clearly, we are all unique individuals and have to be honest enough with ourselves to realize when an interaction or conversation makes us feel closer to a person of the opposite sex than we should allow. Be honest: acknowledge the little thrill you feel when you are flirting, being complimented, or being appreciated for sides of yourself that don't come to the forefront at home. Recognize that housework, childcare, and the stress of work have threatened to turn you and your spouse into drudges and that you're feeling less and less excited about returning home and being with your mate. Don't excuse your behavior with the "everyone does it" attitude. If you're not honest, you'll lose the greatest thing you could have going for you even if your office relationships never lead to sex. However, studies show that 73 percent of men and 42 percent[10] to 57 percent[11] of women meet their extramarital affair partners at work. Keep your coworkers at arm's length.

Where Competition Fails

Another reason for restricting relationships with members of the opposite sex is the danger that competition presents to a marriage. For example, if you stare at airbrushed, naked models in pornographic magazines, you may wonder if the person you're getting into bed with tonight is even of the same species. If you develop a relationship with a member of the opposite sex who has a superior sense of humor to your spouse, you may start to realize how "boring" your spouse really is. Your friendship with others can cause you to see your spouse in a more negative light: "He makes me laugh so much more." "She makes me feel like a man." "He takes much better care of his body." "My spouse doesn't have such a strong work ethic." "My spouse isn't that warm." You begin to judge your spouse based on what you see in your relationships with these other people.

It is unwise and unfair to place this form of competition on your spouse. If you dream of trading in your wife for that Playboy model, remember that a model may spend seven hours a day caring for that body. She may be an insensitive person, a boring or dim companion, a rotten parent, a financially irresponsible spendthrift, or someone who would never find you the least bit attractive.

Similarly, the person you're starting to get close to may have a great sense of humor or be much more "spontaneous" than your spouse but then again, he or she may not have so much of what your spouse has. Maybe he or she doesn't have the same concept of responsibility or warmth or willingness to give to you as your spouse does. Everyone has strengths and weaknesses, and it's unfair to judge your spouse on a specific scale without taking the whole person into account. We aren't slices of bread. It's the whole loaf we have to live and grow with.

There will always be people who possess better parts of a personality than our spouses will. Our spouse will never be the best in every aspect of life. That person doesn't exist. We often think that if our spouse were better at something specific, then we'd have a much better marriage. You may even be convinced that it's healthy to hang out with someone else so you can see what needs to be improved in your own relationship. This form of marital growth doesn't work. Nor do more possessions make the marriage happier or more fulfilled. Paul Wachtel, author of *The Poverty of Affluence,* calls into question our reliance on "more is better" as the solution to all our yearnings.

***

In 1958, when economist John Kenneth Galbraith appropriately described the United States as "The Affluent Society," 95 percent of U.S. households had air conditioning, about 4 percent had dishwashers, and fewer than 15 percent had more than one car. By 1980, when Ronald Reagan's successful bid to replace Jimmy Carter was based on the widespread sense that people were suffering economically, the percentage of homes with air conditioning had quintupled, the percentage of homes with dishwashers had increased more than 700 percent and the percentage with two or more cars had about tripled. Yet, despite the astounding economic growth—despite owning more of the gadgets, machines and appliances thought to constitute "the good life"—Americans felt significantly less well off than they had twenty-two years before, polls showed.[12]

***

No matter what we *have in life, our happiness is largely going to come from within ourselves.* Having a large, elaborately decorated home, expensive cars, multiple vacation homes around the globe, a yacht, and memberships to exclusive clubs and spas offers no added security to your marriage. There is no statistic that declares wealthier couples have better marriages or divorce less.

[10] Glass, as reported in *Chicago Tribune*, August 8, 1999.
[11] Infidelity survey, *New Woman*, October–November, 1986.

[12] Stanley, Thomas J., Ph.D., and Danko, William D., Ph.D. *The Millionaire Next Door* (Longstreet Press, 1996).

The one statistic we have captured is that divorce rates have soared even with all the extra "happy" items we have in our world. Searching to make our spouses measure up to others doesn't lead to happier marriages. It leads to frustration, anger, and conflict. We often overestimate how much pleasure we would receive if our spouses were better in some way. It's much easier to overlook our spouses' weaknesses if we don't create relationships with others to compare them to.

Remember, too, that measuring your spouse against a friend or colleague will always be an incomplete comparison. What's to say that that scintillating conversationalist you admire at work doesn't morph into the same boring partner obsessed with bills and Johnny's orthodonture the second he or she gets home?

A further problem competition brings to a marriage arises when your spouse is trying to change and become a better partner. Let's say you feel that your mate needs to improve his or her listening skills or better understand your feelings—worthy goals. Such goals take time and energy. Ideally, you should appreciate your spouse's efforts even if the change is incremental. However, once you choose to relate to a member of the opposite sex who is better skilled in these areas, it's likely you'll lose patience with your spouse. After all, even though your spouse may be getting better, he or she may still not measure up to your more accomplished friend. If you had never let yourself get involved with this friend, you might be more understanding of your spouse's efforts. More important than any improvement is the fact that your lifemate is showing such caring for you just by focusing on change. It's not all about the new skill, but about the process and experience of growing together. Involvement with someone outside of the marriage can cause you to lose focus on the important parts of your relationship.

This concept of "no competition" may sound odd or extremely limiting to developing a better marriage. My intent is not to make you stagnate but rather to find healthy avenues to improving your marriage. Working and focusing on your marriage means looking at what will make you feel closer to your spouse. There are better ways than flirting and developing a relationship with others to educate yourself. After all, if you wanted to spice up your sex life, would you sleep around and take notes to see what your marriage is missing and learn some new techniques? Of course, you recognize that even if having outside sexual relationships may teach you a thing or two to help your marital sex life, it's clearly stepping out of bounds. But the same is true for sharing your emotional or spiritual self with others. It is just as intimate and as dangerous. Just as you would do to improve your marital sex life, to improve your marital emotional life you need to educate yourself through reading, talking to a mental health professional, or discussing issues with other happily married couples you feel close to.

I can't underscore the importance to any marriage of befriending happily married couples who are openly warm to each other. From such friends you can see different healthy relationship styles. You can go home and say, "I'd like to have more of that spark that they have. Let's try going out one night a week like they do. Let's touch more like they do." Ask other couples for some of the techniques they use to keep their marriage happy. Most every couple that is genuinely happy with their marriage will have plenty of advice because they will have had to work hard themselves at making their marriage satisfying. . . .

***

Ten Rules for Avoiding Emotional Infidelity

1. Keep it all business at the office.
2. Avoid meetings with members of the opposite sex outside of the workplace.
3. Meet in groups.
4. Find polite ways of ending personal conversations.
5. Avoid consistency in the relationship.
6. Don't share your personal feelings.
7. Be unflinchingly honest with yourself.
8. Avoid cordial kisses and hugs, or dancing with members of the opposite sex.
9. Don't drink around the opposite sex.
10. Show your commitment to your spouse daily.

***

So whatever happened to Leon and his on-line romance? After some therapeutic insight, Leon was able to recommit himself to his marriage. After about five months of counseling, he and his wife happily left my office to enjoy the rest of their lives together. About three years later, I received a letter from Leon. He wrote me how well things were and then added, "Remember that woman? You had me put away her envelope and I never looked at it. I guess I never threw it out, and recently upon clearing out some papers, I found it. I couldn't resist looking at it and then sending it your way. It's enclosed."

I opened the envelope and first read the note.

Dear Leon,
It's been wonderful laughing with you. You are a special man, and I wish things were different, but this world isn't meant for us to be together. As you can see, it's neither the time nor the place. Who knows? I'll be satisfied if it works out the next time around.

Love,
Cyber Sal

And there it was. The picture of the woman that brought Leon and his wife's marriage to its knees. The picture revealed a beautiful, gentle-looking woman. On the bottom right-hand corner was written, "74 years old and still hot." Her twisted fingers grasped a cane and her white hair flowed over the top of the recliner she sat on.

***

"It's neither the time nor the place." Sage words from one who has lived a long life. Perhaps all of us can learn from Cyber Sal that when we marry, a good motto for getting involved with others of the opposite sex can be summed up with such a simple phrase. It's neither the time nor the place.

Affairs are not about sex. They are about placing vital marital and life energy into the hands of others who don't deserve them and shouldn't have them. They are about rejecting the commitment and abandoning the love we've offered our spouses. If it's marital bliss you seek, start by knowing that bliss awaits those who respect the importance of commitment.

Emotional Infidelity: How to Avoid It and 10 Other Secrets to a Great Marriage [New York: Crown, 2001], pp. 23–63
Reprinted with permission of the author

Lesson 6
Make Up or Break Up
Negotiating the Most Significant Challenge of Our Generation

Introduction

A discussion of what constitutes grounds for divorce according to the Jewish legal code demonstrates how far one might need to go to make a marriage work. What degree of tolerance can be realistically expected of an individual? When is divorce the best option? And is another's divorce (or marriage) anyone else's business?

Grounds for Marriage
The Tragedy of Divorce

Text 1

כל המגרש את אשתו ראשונה, אפילו מזבח מוריד עליו דמעות, שנאמר (מלאכי
ב,יג), " . . . כסות דמעה את מזבח ה' בכי ואנקה, מאין עוד פנות אל המנחה ולקחת
רצון מידכם". וכתיב (שם יד), "ואמרתם, 'על מה?' על כי ה' העיד בינך ובין אשת
נעוריך אשר אתה בגדתה בה, והיא חברתך ואשת בריתך".

תלמוד בבלי, גיטין צ,ב

Babylonian Talmud. A literary work of monumental proportions that draws upon the totality of the legal, spiritual, intellectual, ethical, and historical traditions of Judaism, the Babylonian Talmud was set up as a commentary to the Mishnah and was written primarily in Aramaic. The Talmud contains the teachings of the Jewish sages, mostly from the period after the destruction of the Second Temple through the fifth century C.E. The Babylonian Talmud has served as the primary vehicle for the education of countless Jews over the centuries; it is the entry point for all subsequent legal, ethical, and theological Jewish scholarship.

When one divorces the wife of his youth, the altar sheds tears, as it is written (Malachi 2:13): ". . . You cover the altar of God with tears, weeping, and sighing; He no longer pays attention to your offering, nor receives it graciously from your hand." The [following] verse continues: "'Why is this?' you ask. Because God is witness between you and the wife of your youth—your companion, the woman with whom you entered a covenant—whom you have betrayed."

Talmud, Gitin 90b

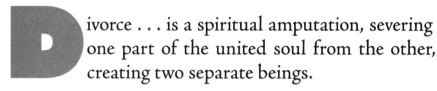

Divorce . . . is a spiritual amputation, severing one part of the united soul from the other, creating two separate beings.

Divorce, like an amputation, is a tragedy, but sometimes it's the right thing to do. Our attitude to divorce parallels our attitude to the amputation of a limb in several ways:

It is painful. When a limb becomes so diseased that it endangers the rest of the body, the patient is faced with a horrible choice: to face the pain of amputation, or risk worse suffering by leaving things as they are. If the future risks are high enough to clearly outweigh the present pain, the right thing to do is cut off the limb. Similarly, divorce is painful for all involved, but it is the right choice when remaining in an unhealthy relationship will only cause more damage, suffering and heartache.

It is a last resort. We do everything possible to avoid needing to amputate. If there is a remote chance that the limb can be salvaged, even with great effort and expense, it is worth a try. Only after exhausting all other possibilities would we resort to amputation. Same with divorce—it is only considered after counseling and sincere efforts to change prove fruitless.

Rabbi Aron Moss teaches Kabbalah, Talmud, and practical Judaism in Sydney, Australia. He serves as rabbi of the Nefesh Synagogue and authors a popular weekly syndicated article on modern Jewish thought.

Rabbi Aron Moss, "What Is the Jewish View on Divorce," www.askmoses.com

How Dispensable Is a Spouse?

Learning Interaction 1

You are a rabbinic scholar and authority on Jewish law, and your mandate is upholding Torah and family values. You also spend considerable time counseling quarreling couples, and, sadly, have seen many a couple divorce over relatively petty issues.

Would you consider enacting a law to help ensure that couples don't divorce over trivialities? If yes, what do you believe should constitute reasonable grounds for divorce?

- ☒ **Irreconcilable differences**
- ❑ **Cruel treatment**
- ❑ **Abandonment**
- ❑ **Adultery**
- ❑ **Mutual agreement to separate**
- ❑ **Other** _____
- ❑ **I would not legislate any grounds. If either spouse insists on divorcing, that should remain his or her prerogative.**

Text 3a 📜

כִּי יִקַּח אִישׁ אִשָּׁה וּבְעָלָהּ, וְהָיָה אִם לֹא תִמְצָא חֵן בְּעֵינָיו כִּי מָצָא בָהּ עֶרְוַת דָּבָר, וְכָתַב
לָהּ סֵפֶר כְּרִיתֻת, וְנָתַן בְּיָדָהּ וְשִׁלְּחָהּ מִבֵּיתוֹ.

דברים כד,א

If a man takes a wife and is intimate with her, and it happens that she does not find favor in his eyes, for he discovers in her an immoral matter, then he writes for her a bill of divorce, places it into her hand, and sends her away from his house.

Deuteronomy 24:1

Text 3b 📜

בית שמאי אומרים, לא יגרש אדם את אשתו אלא אם כן מצא בה דבר ערוה, שנאמר,
"כי מצא בה ערות דבר".
ובית הלל אומרים, אפילו הקדיחה תבשילו, שנאמר, "כי מצא בה ערות דבר".
רבי עקיבא אומר, אפילו מצא אחרת נאה הימנה, שנאמר, "והיה אם לא תמצא חן
בעיניו".

תלמוד בבלי גיטין צ,א

The School of Shamai taught: A man ought not divorce his wife unless she is guilty of immoral misconduct, as it is stated, "Because he discovers in her an immoral matter."

The School of Hillel taught: [A man may divorce his wife] even if she burned his dish, as it is stated, "Because

---

lesson **6**   make up or break up   **151**

he discovers in her an immoral [act, or any other malicious] matter."

Rabbi Akiva says: [A man may divorce his wife] even if he found another more attractive than she, as it is stated, "And it happens that she does not find favor in his eyes."

Talmud, Gitin 90a

Question for Discussion

Can you propose a way to reconcile the traditional Jewish view of divorce with the opinions of Rabbi Akiva and the School of Hillel?

Text 4

בכל ספר מלאכי כתיב "ה' צבאות", ובכאן כתיב "אלקי ישראל", שנאמר, (מלאכי ב,טז), "כי שנא שלח, אמר ה' אלהי ישראל".
כביכול לא יחול שמו אלא על ישראל בלבד.
בראשית רבה, יח,ה

Bereishit Rabah is an early rabbinic commentary on the Book of Genesis, bearing the name of Rabbi Oshiya Rabah (Rabbi Oshiya "the Great") whose teaching opens this work. This *midrash* provides textual exegeses and stories, expounds upon the biblical narrative, and develops and illustrates moral principles. Thought to be the earliest non-halachic *midrash* extant, it was produced by the sages of the Talmud in the Land of Israel, its Aramaic closely resembling that of the Jerusalem Talmud. It was first published in Constantinople in 1512 together with four other midrashic works on the other four books of the Pentateuch.

In the entire book of Malachi, [God is referred to as] the "Lord of hosts," but [when it discusses divorce, God is referred to as] "the God of Israel"; as it says (Malachi 2:16), "If you despise her, send her away—so says the God of Israel."

This teaches us that God's Name is only associated, as it were, with Jewish [divorce].

Midrash, *Bereishit Rabah* 18:5

The Case for Divorce

Text 5

אין אדם דר עם נחש בכפיפה.

תלמוד בבלי, כתובות עב,א

A person cannot live together with a snake in one basket.

Talmud, Ketubot 72a

Free to Stay

Text 6

השתא שרי לשבחא לה: "לזאת יקרא אשה' (בראשית ב,כג)—דא היא דלא ישתכח
כוותיה, דא היא יקרא דביתא, כלהון נשין גבה כקופא בפני בני נשא. אבל לזאת יקרא
אשה, שלימו דכלא, לזאת ולא לאחרא".

זהר א, מט,ב

Adam began to sing Eve's praises: "'This shall be called woman' (Genesis 2:23)—this is the peerless one; this is the pride of the house, who surpasses all other women as a human being surpasses an ape. This one is perfect in all points, and she alone merits the title of woman."

Zohar 1:49b

Zohar. The most seminal work of Kabbalah, Jewish mysticism. It is a mystical commentary on the Torah, written in Aramaic and Hebrew. According to Arizal, the Zohar consists of the teachings of Rabbi Shimon bar Yocha'i who lived in the Land of Israel during the 2nd century. The Zohar has become one of the indispensable texts of traditional Judaism, alongside and nearly equal in stature to the Mishnah and Talmud.

שמא תאמר עשוי הוא היתר הגירושין לרופף את ברית הנשואין ולהפריד בין הדבקים ולהטיל מוראו בכל שעת קטטה ומריבה שבין איש לאשתו? אין הדבר כן, אלא היתר הגירושין בישראל חיזוק גדול הוא לברית הנשואין, שהוא עושה את הדבק ביניהם שיהא דבק טוב מרצון ולא מאונס . . .

כל נתיבותיה שלום (משלי ג,יג)—אפילו זה שדומה בעיניך כאילו יש בה פירוד. אף משפט הגט לא ניתן אלא לשלום הבריות ולמען שלמות המשפחה . . .

רק הסר נא דאגה זו מלבם והשב להם שלוותם, לידע כי חרותם לא נטלה מהם מכל וכל . . . לא יאבדו עולמם בשעה אחת של חרון אף אלא ישבו בשלוה ויצפו לזעם שיעבורו. נמצא שאפילו בשעה שאהבתם פגומה—חייהם חיי רצון ולא חיי אונס וזעם. מה הוא הדבר שמרגיעם בשעת כעסם? הווה אומר: דבר זה שאמרו חכמים: אפילו מצא אחרת נאה הימנה רשאי הוא לגרשה!

משל, למה הדבר דומה? לאחד שהמלכות גזרה עליו שישב כלוא בביתו. עדיין לא עבר עליו יום אחד בכלאו והריהו יושב בביתו ומצטער. שמא תאמר אדם זה קשה לו ישיבתו בתוך ביתו? והרי כמה וכמה פעמים שראינוהו מסתגר בתוך ביתו וישב בו להנאתו ימים אחדים ומתענג בו. אמור מעתה: לא ביתו גורם לצערו אלא הגזירה גורמת; נוטל אתה את הגזירה, הרי הוא יושב במקומו ומתענג.

איש וביתו, ע′ 62–68

One might think that the allowance for divorce weakens the marriage institution, for the fear of divorce will loom large whenever the husband and wife quarrel or fight. This is not so. Paradoxically, the allowance for divorce strengthens marriage; it makes for a beautiful union—a union that stands upon the free will of its parties, not coercion. . . .

"All the [Torah's] pathways are peaceful" (Proverbs 3:13). Even the law of divorce, which is seemingly intended to create separation, is actually intended to engender peace and preserve the integrity of the family unit. . . .

[The Torah] removes the worry from the heart and restores peoples' serenity, for they are assured in the knowledge that their freedom has not at all been taken from them.... Hence, they will not destroy their lives in a fit of anger; rather they will remain at peace and wait out the stressful moments in marriage. What calms them in their moments of anger? That which the sages said: "Even if he finds another more beautiful than she, he *may* divorce her."

This is like a person placed under house arrest. One day of his incarceration has yet to pass, and there he is, sitting in his home, completely miserable. Is it because he finds staying in his home unbearable? That cannot be so, because on many previous occasions he was observed not leaving his home for several days at a time, and he enjoyed and relished that private time! It is clear that it is not staying at home that is so distressing to him, but being coerced to do so. In the absence of the coercion, he would happily sit in his home.

Rabbi Avraham Eliyahu Kitov, *Ish Ubeito*, pp. 62–68

Rabbi Avraham Eliyahu Kitov (1912–1976). Educator and community activist, he was born in Warsaw, Poland, and settled in Israel in 1936. Employed in the construction industry, he helped establish the Union of Agudath Israel Workers to help its members find employment; he also served as editor of its newspaper. As an educator, he dedicated much of his life to writing. Some of his notable works include *Ish Ubeito* and *Sefer Hatoda'ah*, both of which have been translated into English.

The Wedding of the Millennium

Text 8

כל המשים שלום בתוך ביתו, מעלה עליו הכתוב כאילו משים שלום בישראל על כל
אחד ואחד.
וכל המטיל קנאה ותחרות בתוך ביתו, מעלה עליו הכתוב כאילו מטיל קנאה ותחרות
בישראל.

אבות דרבי נתן כח,ג

Avot DeRabbi Natan is a commentary on, and an elaboration of, the mishnaic tractate Avot, bearing the name of Rabbi Natan, one of the sages of the Mishnah (late 2nd century C.E.). The work exists in two very different versions. Since 1550, one of these versions has been printed in the standard editions of the Talmud.

God considers those who bring peace to their homes as if they brought peace to the entire nation of Israel and to every single individual.

God considers those who create strife and enmity in their homes as if they created strife and enmity among the entire nation of Israel.

Avot DeRabbi Natan 28:3

שָׁלוֹם

Text 9

ברוך אתה ה׳ . . . אשר ברא ששון ושמחה, חתן וכלה. גילה, רנה, דיצה, וחדוה, אהבה, ואחוה, שלום, ורעות. מהרה ה׳ אלקינו ישמע בערי יהודה ובחוצות ירושלים: קול ששון וקול שמחה, קול חתן וקול כלה, קול מצהלות חתנים מחפתם ונערים ממשתה נגינתם.

נוסח שבע ברכות

Blessed are You, God . . . Who created joy and happiness; groom and bride; gladness, jubilation, cheer, and delight; love, friendship, harmony, and fellowship. O God, let there speedily be heard in the streets of Jerusalem the sound of joy and the sound of happiness, the sound of a groom and the sound of a bride, the sound of exultation of grooms from under their wedding canopies and youths from their joyous banquets.

Text of *Sheva Berachot*

Text 10

העולם הזה אירוסין היו . . . אבל לימות המשיח יהיו נישואין, שנאמר (ישעיה נד,ה), "כי בועליך עושיך".

שמות רבה טו,לא

This world is like a betrothal [period between God and Israel]. The wedding will take place in the Messianic era, as it says (Isaiah 54:5), "For your Maker will be your husband."

Midrash, *Shemot Rabah* 15:31

Shemot Rabah is an early rabbinic commentary of the Book of Exodus. This *midrash,* written mostly in Hebrew, provides textual exegeses and stories, expounds upon the biblical narrative, and develops and illustrates moral principles. It was first published in Constantinople in 1512 together with four other midrashic works on the other four books of the Pentateuch.

Text 11 📖

שית אלפי שני הוו עלמא.

תלמוד בבלי, סנהדרין צז,א

The world will last for six thousand years [after which it will enter the Messianic era].

Talmud, Sanhedrin 97a

Text 12 📖

ואם בכל עת הפליגו רבותינו זכרונם לברכה במעלת השלום בית, על אחת כמה וכמה בערב שבת קדש. ואנו עתה כולנו בתוך כלל ישראל בערב שבת קדש לאחר חצות, שקרב קץ גלותנו וביאת משיח צדקנו.

מובן שההעלם וההסתר ביותר הוא בנוגע לשלום בית, כי ידוע שגדול השלום וכל התורה כולה דרכיה דרכי נועם וכל נתיבותיה שלום, ובפרט בגלות זה האחרון שכמאמר רבותינו זכרונם לברכה ביומא ט' ע"ב בא בסיבת העדר השלום, וכל כמה שמתקרב קץ הגלות הרי ההתאבקות מצד שכנגד הוא ביותר בנוגע שלא להניח לעשות שלום בעולם בכלל ובין איש ואשתו דלמטה שלהם בדוגמת איש ואשה דלמעלה בפרט.

אבל לפום גמלא שיחנא, ובודאי נותנים הכחות על זה לעמוד בנסיון.

אגרות קודש כ"ק אדמו"ר זי"ע, ח"ד, ע' תלג

If at all times, our sages, of blessed memory, spoke of the extreme importance of preserving marital harmony, how much more so this pertains to the eve of the holy Sabbath. We and our entire nation now stand on the eve of the holy Sabbath after midday, for the end of our exile and the coming of Mashiach is imminent.

Maintaining marital harmony is so challenging because of the great importance of peace—to the extent that regarding the entire Torah it is said, "Its ways are pleasant ways and all its pathways are peaceful." Preserving peace is particularly [important, and thus] challenging in our present exile, which our sages tell us (Talmud, Yoma 9b) was caused by a lack of peace. As we approach the end of this exile, the [unholy forces of the] "other side" exert great effort to ensure that peace does not prevail—in the world at large, and especially between husband and wife, who correspond to the supernal husband and wife [i.e., God and Israel].

Nevertheless, "the camel is only loaded with a burden that is in accordance with its strength" (Talmud, Sotah 13b). Hence, we are certainly provided [by God] with the powers necessary to successfully meet this great challenge.

The Lubavitcher Rebbe, Rabbi Menachem Mendel Schneerson, *Igrot Kodesh* 4:433

Rabbi Menachem Mendel Schneerson (1902–1994). Known as "the Lubavitcher Rebbe," or simply as "the Rebbe." Born in southern Ukraine, Rabbi Schneerson escaped Nazi-occupied Europe, arriving in the U.S. in June 1941. The towering Jewish leader of the 20th century, the Rebbe inspired and guided the revival of traditional Judaism after the European devastation, impacting virtually every Jewish community the world over. The Rebbe often emphasized that the performance of just one additional good deed could usher in the era of Mashiach. The Rebbe's scholarly talks and writings have been printed in more than 200 volumes.

If You're Not Part of the Solution . . .

Text 13

ומה שמבהיל אותי ביותר הוא זה שכותב שנמצאת אחותו בבית הוריה.
אשר לדאבוננו ראינו במוחש שכשמתערבים בין איש לאשתו אפילו הקרובים ביותר.
(ולפעמים הרי יש חשש יותר להיזק חס ושלום מאשר לתיקון דוקא הקרובים, בהיותם
צד וקרוב לאחד מהנזכרים לעיל, יש מקום להיזק יותר מהתערבות של זר).
שם, ח"י, ע' נח

From your letter, I find it particularly alarming that your sister is currently staying in her parents' home.

Sadly, we have clearly seen [the disastrous consequences] of people mixing into matters that are between husband and wife. This is true even if those who intervene are very close to the affected parties.

(At times, the intervention of those who are close to one of the parties has greater potential to cause damage. Inasmuch as they are very close to one of the spouses, there is greater possibility for damage, more so than when a stranger intervenes.)

The Lubavitcher Rebbe, Rabbi Menachem M. Schneerson, ibid., 10:58

Text 14a 📖

גדול השלום, שאף הקדוש ברוך הוא שינה בו, דמעיקרא כתיב (בראשית יח,יב),
"ואדוני זקן", ולבסוף כתיב (שם יג), "ואני זקנתי".

תלמוד בבלי, יבמות סה,ב

Peace is so important that even God modified a statement for the sake of peace: Originally it is written [that Sarah said], "My husband is old" (Genesis 18:12); afterwards, however, [when God repeated Sarah's statement to Abraham,] it is written, "and I am old" (ibid., 18:13).

Talmud, Yevamot 65b

Text 14b 📖

הוי מתלמידיו של אהרן, אוהב שלום ורודף שלום.

משנה, אבות א,יב

Be a disciple of Aaron, who was a lover of peace and a pursuer of peace.

Mishnah, Avot 1:12

Mishnah. The first authoritative work of Jewish law—in addition to the biblical books—that was codified in writing, it consists of the oral traditions that were passed down from teacher to student. Due to the perpetual persecution of the Jewish people, it became increasingly difficult to guarantee that the oral traditions would not be forgotten. Therefore, Rabbi Yehudah Hanasi, at the end of the second century, redacted the Mishnah. The Mishnah supplements, complements, clarifies, and systematizes the commandments of the Torah. It is the central literary document that serves as the foundation for both the Jerusalem Talmud and the Babylonian Talmud.

Text 15a 📖

One day, when I was walking down the street with one of my teachers, we were approached by a young couple. The wife said to my teacher, "Isn't it true that stirring the soup while it's on the stove would violate the Sabbath? Tell my husband— he doesn't know!"

My teacher looked thoughtful for a minute and said, "I'll have to look it up and get back to you." The couple went on.

Then, noticing my puzzled expression, my teacher explained, "You're surprised at my answer, because the wife's question was such a simple one. You and I both know that she was correct. But for me to have known the answer without so much as a glance at the *Code of Jewish Law* would have made her husband appear foolish."

My teacher had wisely chosen to allow himself to appear foolish, rather than diminish a husband in his wife's eyes. Why? Because marriage is sacred. To do anything that diminishes it, discourages it, or dulls it is wrong. To say something discouraging or disparaging about a husband to a wife, about a wife to a husband, is an unpardonable sin. . . .

Rabbi Manis Friedman, *Doesn't Anyone Blush Anymore* [S. Francisco: HarperSanFrancisco, 1990], pp. 25–26

Rabbi Manis Friedman (1946–) is a renowned author, counselor, lecturer, and philosopher. He hosts his own cable television series, *Torah Forum with Manis Friedman*, which is syndicated throughout North America. More than 150,000 copies of his thought-provoking and entertaining video and audio tapes have been sold. He is the author of *Doesn't Anyone Blush Anymore?* and the founder and dean of Bais Chana Institute of Jewish Studies in Minnesota.

Text 15b

To come to a wife and say derogatory things about her husband is unconscionable; by the same token, to come to the husband and say nasty things about his wife is intolerable. But, unknowingly, we often find ourselves doing just that.

At a party or family gathering, for example, we may be so charming and witty that everyone else pales by comparison. In this way, although it is unintentional, we may make a husband look bad in the presence of his wife, or make a wife look bad in the presence of her husband. We must be aware of this possibility.

One of the holiest acts is to bring peace between a husband and wife. This doesn't mean that if the husband and wife are fighting, we ought to referee the fight. That would bring a ceasefire, but it wouldn't bring peace.

Bringing peace to a husband and wife means that on every occasion, whenever we have the chance, we should enhance the husband's opinion of his wife and the wife's opinion of her husband. Help the husband appreciate his wife, and the wife respect her husband—before there's a problem, as my teacher did. That helps to prevent the problem. That's what is meant by promoting peace, not a ceasefire between husband and wife.

Rabbi Manis Friedman, ibid., pp. 26–27

Key Points

1. Inasmuch as a husband and wife constitute one complete being, divorce is analogous to an amputation; it is considered a tragedy and should only be employed as a last resort.

2. Nevertheless, the Torah allows divorce for several reasons, including: one should not be compelled to live in an abusive situation; without the possibility of divorce, spouses would have less incentive to work on their marriages; true love cannot flourish in a state of coercion.

3. The relationship of every husband and wife is a reflection of the relationship between God and His people. When husband and wife live in harmony, they engender harmony between the Jewish people and God, leading to the grand cosmic wedding that will take place during the Messianic era.

4. Today, as we stand on the threshold of the Messianic redemption, maintaining marital harmony is a particularly difficult challenge, inasmuch as so much hinges on our success in this area.

5. Because the entire Jewish nation has a vested interest in the success of every individual marriage, every person is responsible to do all he or she can to help others enhance their marriages.

6. When supporting a friend or relative through a marital rough patch, it is vital not to undermine the marriage or demean the friend's spouse.

7. Through helping others with their marriages, our own marriages are also enhanced.

Additional Readings

The Marriage Meeting Program

by **Marcia Naomi Berger**

The morning blessings provide a daily reminder of the mitzvah to bring peace between a husband and wife. Most couples can maintain *sholom bayis* [marital harmony] with a practical, easy-to-implement system: the Marriage Meeting Program.

Couples who conduct Marriage Meetings report a twenty to eighty percent increase in happiness with their relationship, as indicated by follow-up studies of people who learned the technique at one of my workshops or private psychotherapy sessions in my San Rafael, California, office. One woman from Brooklyn learned it by telephone, and later said the meetings "turned my marriage around." Marriage meetings foster a loving connection, teamwork, and respectful resolution of conflicts.

Typically men are more likely than their wives to resist scheduling a meeting, but once they try one, they are pleased with the results. One husband said this approach is "direct, refreshing, and sorely needed." Another stated that when his wife urged him to try a meeting, he was petrified, but he went along with it, was very pleased with the results, and he planned to keep scheduling meetings. Personally, I can vouch for Marriage Meetings. My husband and I have been holding them for twenty-one years, having started as newlyweds. I cannot imagine a better way to keep a relationship on track.

Here is how a Marriage Meeting works:

The meeting has a four-part agenda: ***Appreciation, Chores, Plan for Good Times***, and ***Problems and Challenges***. Set a time limit of 45 minutes to decrease the likelihood of fatigue. Meet when both of you are alert, not tired or hungry. Try meeting in your living room with your appointment books nearby. Avoid any interruptions. After you have established a routine, you can experiment by meeting in different settings.

The ***Appreciation*** part of the meeting comes first. Each partner takes a turn, saying specific things he or she appreciated about the other during the week. A few Do's and Don'ts to keep this part of the meeting flowing smoothly:

Do use "I statements" here and throughout the meeting, as "I appreciate your calling me to say you'd be late getting home, and your greeting me with a smile when you came in."

Do remember to express appreciation for positive character traits, such as, "I appreciate your patience in listening to my complaints about my job."

Do tell each other what you like that they've done to help make your home a peaceful sanctuary, whether this means keeping the appliances in working order by scheduling needed repairs, attending parenting classes, or engaging in other activities that bring out the best in each of you.

Don't omit the obvious. Everyone wants to know, for example, that his or her financial contributions to the marriage are appreciated, that their spouse finds them physically attractive, etc.

Don't criticize. Stick with appreciation during this part of the meeting, even if sometimes the considerate phone call doesn't happen.

Don't fall into the trap, when miffed at your partner, of thinking there is nothing to appreciate. What about the time he picked up the children from school? Took out the garbage? And...

What else might you be taking for granted? How about the time he cooked your favorite dinner? Or that moment when she looked across the room at you and smiled? Or when he visited your aunt with you? That was kind, wasn't it? Tell him! Tell her!

Some of us hesitate to express appreciation. Do it anyway. Even if you blush! Before the meeting, write down a few things you want to mention so you won't forget. Stay with the positive. As you conclude your complimentary remarks, ask, "Did I leave anything out?" Your spouse may reply, "Did you appreciate that I picked your mother up at the airport last Sunday?" Of course! You appreciated that too. How could you have forgotten? You both smile, feeling pretty good about now, and ready to continue with the meeting's agenda.

The **Chores** topic comes next. Each of you says what needs to be done, and reports on what you have done. It's easy to feel overwhelmed about all the tasks on one's "to-do" list. Keep it simple with these Do's and Don'ts:

Do list chores and agree on who is responsible for doing each, along with timelines. For example, if it's time to replace the toaster-oven, one of you mentions this. Either one of you can offer to pick up a new one by Thursday, or within any mutually agreeable time.

Do set priorities together, once the list is complete, so that what's important to each of you will get done soon.

Do put some chores on hold to make time for higher priorities. New linoleum for the kitchen can wait until after the leaky roof gets repaired or replaced. The checkbook can get balanced after the tax receipts are organized.

Don't wallow in guilt because you wish you'd taken care of something sooner, just move it up to the top of your "to-do" list.

Don't criticize. Maybe he says he'll fill out the forms for your child's new school by next week but you don't believe him, knowing his past record. Zip your lip and accept his good intention; progress reports will follow at future meetings.

Don't waste energy blaming yourself either for something you haven't done yet.

You will like knowing that your priorities are mutual, that you two are not working at cross-purposes. So if your home needs repairs, money needs management, or a wedding gift needs to be bought, when you both take care of business, each of you feels good.

Sometimes discussion about a chore becomes emotional, such as when one partner is feeling very upset with the other about something relating to a chore. Instead of saying something like, "I'm tired of having to remind you so often to ....," save this part of the conversation for the last part of the meeting: *Problems and Challenges*. Keep the discussion around chores crisp, positive, and business-like.

Plan for Good Times follows the *Chores* part of a Marriage Meetings. Plans take energy; good times restore us, recharge our batteries. What if it's been so long since you've planned any enjoyable activities that you think you've forgotten how to have a good time? Perhaps you'd like a bubble bath or a workout at the gym. A walk in the woods, a visit to a friend? A watercolor class you'd like to take? Would you enjoy camping or a different sort of vacation? Some Do's and Don'ts:

Do take time to think of activities you enjoy.

Do plan good times for yourself, dates with your partner, and family outings.

Don't fall into the martyr trap. You feel guilty about taking time for yourself? The happiness you feel after investing time in yourself will reverberate to your partner and children.

Don't forget to plan vacations—sometimes a getaway for the two of you, other times for the whole family.

Problems and Challenges, the last part of the meeting, is the time to bring up any issue for discussion. It can feel intimidating to say what's on our minds, not knowing how the other person will respond. Speak up anyway! This is the time to clear the air and seek solutions.

You love the idea of overnight guests, but you're feeling exhausted from having had so many lately. Talk it out and remember to use "I" statements, such as, "I want to do the mitzvah of *hachnosis orchim* (hospitality to guests) but I'm exhausted from how much overnight company we've had recently." Maybe it's time to say no to potential guests for a while; alternatively, it may work fine to have them if others will agree to pitch in more to help with the extra chores. Together, work towards a solution.

This is the time to talk about changing needs, transitions, and intimacy concerns. How will a new work or volunteer schedule affect your routines and relationship? Are you considering having an elderly relative come to live with you? Does one of you want more intimacy or crave more alone time? Concerned about money? What new challenges are you anticipating? Keep talking.

Do start small. Try to keep this part of the meeting light the first few times by bringing up only issues that are fairly easy to resolve. Once you have established a pattern of successful meetings, you can move on to more sensitive matters.

Do use "I" statements. They help prevent the listener from feeling criticized.

Do speak up, even if you are afraid of how your partner may respond.

Do brainstorm for solutions. List and consider a number of alternatives until one emerges that works for both of you.

Don't allow yourself to feel overwhelmed by big, seemingly unsolvable problems. Change takes time, especially for the bigger issues. Change takes time; be patient with the process.

Don't blame. Attack the problem—not each other!

An example of an easy problem for an early meeting: Ask your partner if he or she is happy with the meals you're preparing or whether something different is preferred, such as more vegetarian and fewer meat meals, or similar meals but with less oil, sugar, or salt. The

answer is likely to emerge in the same meeting. Some of the more emotionally charged issues mentioned above may take weeks or months, or even longer to resolve.

One of you may be more motivated to schedule meetings than the other. One partner may have a stronger need for closure than the other, feeling stymied when unresolved issues are allowed to fester. If that sounds like you, understand both your need and your partner's reluctance. Either way, express appreciation to your spouse for participating. Do something pleasurable right after the meeting; this can be as simple as a handshake or a sharing a special dessert.

End the meeting on a positive note. Jerusalem wasn't built in a day; not every issue will be resolved immediately. Appreciate yourselves for hanging in there together and be confident about the process. Solutions will emerge in time.

To summarize, the structure of Marriage Meetings helps each partner to feel accepted, appreciated, and heard by the other. It offers an assurance that virtually any issue can be discussed effectively and resolved over time, if not immediately. The meetings provide a supportive environment for the airing of different opinions. Regardless of how much any couple has in common, each partner is an individual with a unique personality, wants, and needs. While some people try to whitewash conflicts that defy their fantasy of "togetherness," I believe that noticing your differences is crucial, and that doing so helps to keep a relationship thriving, so long as your differences are accepted in the positive spirit that well-conducted meetings generate.

Some of those differences are exactly what attracted you to each other in the first place, right? If you think your relationship has deteriorated to the point where a Marriage Meeting wouldn't be feasible, consider consulting a psychotherapist skilled in working with couples who can provide you with tools to improve your communications.

But try a meeting anyway—you never know. Regardless of how good you may feel about your relationship, there is always room to grow. Wouldn't you like to have a special time to hear how your partner appreciates you, to plan good times, to organize chores, and to address challenges successfully?

Forty-five minutes. A small investment for a huge return.

Marcia Naomi Berger, MSW, LCSW, has a private psychotherapy practice based in San Rafael, California. She is the author of the Marriage Meeting Starter Kit. *An instructor for continuing education classes for therapists, she serves on the faculties of the University of California Berkeley Extension and Alliant International University in San Francisco.*

Reprinted with permission of the author

What If You Mess Up? What Divorce Teaches About Marriage

by **Rabbi Manis Friedman**

Why does G-d tell you how to get divorced, if He believes in marriage?

Not only does He believe in marriage, He believes that you should be married, and He wants you to be married to the person you are married to.

Why, then, does He allow you to get divorced? Not only allows it, but tells you how to do it?

As with all G-d's instructions in the Torah, getting divorced is a mitzvah, a divine commandment. In fact, His instructions on divorce are very explicit. But why?

Because, having said what His instructions for marriage are, G-d doesn't abandon you when you get in trouble.

Because He is merciful and compassionate, kind and considerate, He gives you a second set of instructions, in case you can't follow the first set.

That's like a cookbook that tells you what to do if you ruin the recipe. Two of my children were once following the instructions on a package of cookie mix. One of them read the instructions aloud, while the other prepared the mix. The child who was reading said, "Now you're supposed to stir the dough fifty times." The other one exclaimed, "But I'm already up to a hundred! What do we do now?"

So the first child said, "I don't know. I'll go back and see what it says to do." He checked the box, but the instructions didn't say anything about stirring the dough too many times. The two of them came to me and asked what they should do. "Should we throw it out? Should we start all over? The instructions don't tell us what to do if we mess up."

G-d isn't like that. That's not how Torah—His set of instructions—is written. He tells you what to do if you ruin the recipe.

It's as though G-d says to you, "This is the person I have selected for you. This is the person I want you to be married to. You can't? It hurts too much? Then don't. Leave. But when you do, please shut the door behind you."

So He not only tells us we may get divorced, He tells us how. "Here is the divine commandment for how to get in, and here is another divine commandment for how to get out."

G-d talks to us that way because He's married to us.

Like everything else that exists in this world, marriage is a reflection of what exists in the spiritual world. There is an absolute marriage that exists between G-d and us.

Marriage requires that something which you take seriously and strictly upon yourself, you are very lenient and accommodating about with your partner. G-d is married to us, and that He takes very seriously. He is committed to the relationship. Therefore, He is lenient and accommodating when we don't always live up to His expectations.

G-d says to us: "You messed up? Then try again. You blew it? Then here is what you have to do. You forgot?

Then next time, try to remember. You forgot a second time? Try a third time." That's how we know that He's committed to the marriage.

Sometimes G-d does even better than that. He asks us what our intentions were. For instance, He tells us not to mix meat and milk. What happens if we do? "Well," He says, "it depends on how much milk there was, and how much meat there was. And did you do it on purpose? Or was it an accident? If it was an accident, this is how you fix it. If it was on purpose, try not to let it happen again."

G-d expects you to be married, and to the person He has chosen for you. But He is compassionate and understanding when you tell Him that it's just too difficult.

Maybe He intended for you to get married and then get out; maybe the laws for divorce are your "escape clause."

No.

G-d intends for you to stay married. But if you can't, if it's too difficult for you, He understands, and He will help you out.

Does that mean your marriage was a mistake? You took a gamble, you lost, now admit it and get out? You made a mistake, so G-d is telling you how to fix it?

Wrong again.

Your marriage wasn't a mistake. It was intended since the beginning of time. When G-d created your soul, six thousand years ago, He created your "intended" along with you.

Saying that you married the wrong person is like saying you gave birth to the wrong baby. Could you have somebody else's baby? A woman once said something like that to me. "You have how many children?" she asked, incredulously. I don't remember how many we had at that time, maybe ten or twelve.

"Don't you know there are some people who can't have children?" She was indignant. It was as if she were saying, "Give somebody else a break. Share a little. Don't have so many kids; let other people have a few." It doesn't happen like that. You don't give birth to someone else's children. The children that you have were meant to be yours.

As Einstein said, "G-d doesn't play dice with the universe." If G-d doesn't play dice with atoms or molecules, then He doesn't play dice with hearts or minds or souls.

You are married to the person you are intended to be married to. G-d arranged it. He set it up; He predestined it from the beginning. In other words, His mind is made up that that's the way He wants it.

You don't want it? Fine. Since He is married to you, He says, "Whatever you want."

Will it spoil "some vast eternal plan," as Tevye asks in *Fiddler on the Roof*? The answer is yes. Yes, if you get divorced, you will spoil some vast eternal plan— G-d's plan. But will He let you? Will He help you? Yes, He will let you, and He will help you.

The reason that G-d allows divorce, and commands divorce, is because by doing so, He is teaching you how to be married.

So even though G-d has rules, even though He has laws, even though He has divine commandments, when you sin, He tells you: "You messed up? Try again. You made a mistake and you admit it? Don't worry about it; you'll do better next time. You did it ten times already? Ask for forgiveness, and I'll forgive you ten times."

That's exactly how you should be married—by treating your spouse the way G-d treats you. With that much mercy and compassion, that much kindness and consideration.

Your wife did it to you again? Forgive her again. She did it ten times? Forgive her ten times.

Be as committed to making this relationship last as G-d has been committed to making His relationship with you last. The moral is, by offering to help you get divorced, G-d is helping you stay married for all time. The way He has stayed married to you.

Rabbi Manis Friedman is a world-renowned author, counselor, lecturer and philosopher; and co-founder of Bais Chana Institute of Jewish Studies in Minnesota. He also served as simultaneous translator for the live televised talks by the Lubavitcher Rebbe.

Reprinted with permission of The Judaism Website—Chabad.org

Marital Harmony

Select letters by the Lubavitcher Rebbe, Rabbi Menachem Mendel Schneerson, of righteous memory, on the subject of marital harmony.

You surely know the tremendous importance of peace and harmony among Jews, as is so often emphasized in our Torah.

The Torah is even more emphatic about Shalom Bayis, peace and harmony in the relationship between husband and wife. So much so that, despite the sanctity of every word in the Torah, especially the sanctity of G-d's name inscribed in the Torah, there is one occasion when G-d Himself orders His written name to be effaced by water, and that is... in order to preserve the peaceful relationship between husband and wife.

In light of the above you will find my answer to your question, which is that you ought to try your utmost not only to preserve a peaceful and harmonious relationship with your husband, but even to strengthen it and, as in every area of the desirable and good, to the point where it will serve as an inspiring example to all those around you.

Needless to say, I am not attempting to make a judgment as to who is right and who is wrong, who is at fault, and to what extent, etc., etc. But even assuming, for the sake of argument, that one of you is entirely in the right,

it is still very worthwhile to do everything possible for the sake of Shalom Bayis.

Moreover, as the wisest of all men said, "As water mirrors the face to the face so does the heart of man to man."[1] It is certain then, that a consistently friendly and conciliatory attitude on your part is bound to evoke reciprocal feeling on the part of your husband.

Excerpted from a letter written in 1974; *Eternal Joy: A Guide to Shidduchim & Marriage* [Brooklyn, N.Y.: Sichos in English, 2000], 3:80

***

In reply to your letter from Sunday, which, because of its important content, I hasten to answer:

You write about the relations and interactions between husbands and wives, etc.

Considering the teaching of our sages of blessed memory[2] that the reward for bringing peace between husband and wife is that one "enjoys the fruits [in this world, while the main reward comes in the World to Come]," it is clear that any and all efforts [in the endeavor of restoring marital harmony] are worthwhile.

It is also clear that, in matters such as these, it is impossible to provide hard and fast rules, for any advice given would depend on the personality of the husband and wife as well as the nature of their environment.

However, it is also certain that each and every individual can indeed be approached and [constructively] influenced.

[This can be accomplished] when a person reflects in order to determine the proper manner by which he can influence this particular individual, approaching him time and again in a pleasant manner, but with firmness and with words that emanate from the heart.

---

[1] Proverbs 27:19.

[2] Talmud, Shabbat 127a.

All the above is not difficult to convey in a heartfelt manner, for marital harmony is of tremendous importance to both husband and wife, as well as to all future generations that will issue from them.

In such instances, it is beneficial to conduct oneself in the manner of Aaron, the "Lover of Peace," as described in the 12th chapter of *Avot DeRabbi Natan*.

May G-d bless you with success in [your efforts to] help create a stable house in Israel, and that these efforts be grounded in Torah and mitzvot. . . .

If the careers of the above-mentioned couple permit, it is quite possible that their traveling together for a few weeks to a vacation spot for a second honeymoon would rectify the entire situation.

Excerpted and translated from a letter, November 7, 1960; *Igrot Kodesh* 20:19

Acknowledgments

"How goodly are your tents, O Jacob, your dwelling places, O Israel." (Numbers 24:5)

SINCE TIME IMMEMORIAL, a strong family unit, based on the solid foundation of strong marriages, has been a primary source of our nation's strength and resilience. Our grandparents looked to the Torah for the wisdom and perspective necessary to keep the colors and hues of marriage sharp and lustrous. This wisdom was taught in the halls of Torah academies, but more importantly, was conveyed from father to son, mother to daughter—verbally and via personal example. The current course, *The Art of Marriage,* is a brave attempt to distill and adapt these age-old teachings, making them resonant for a 21st-century audience.

This course is based on a marriage seminar developed by **Rabbi Nissan Dovid Dubov**, a renowned scholar who has authored more than ten books on Jewish law and Kabbalah, and director for nearly a quarter of a century of Chabad Lubavitch in Wimbledon, UK. Rabbi Dubov has many years of experience in providing premarital therapy and helping countless married couples jumpstart stagnant or tumultuous marriages. We consider ourselves very fortunate to have benefited from Rabbi Dubov's wisdom and guidance.

The JLI Editorial Board has provided many useful suggestions to enhance the course and ensure its suitability for a wide range of students. Many thanks to **Rabbis Hesh Epstein, Sholom Raichik, Shraga Sherman,** and **Motti Wilhelm** for their careful review.

We are greatly indebted to **Rabbis Mordechai Dinerman** and **Naftali Silberberg,** who capably head the JLI Curriculum Department and the Flagship editorial team. **Rabbi Dovid Markel** greatly assisted in the editorial process of this course and **Rabbi Michoel Rivkin** provided research assistance.

Dr. Chana Silberstein provided the editorial vision and direction for this course, which reflects her remarkable understanding of the art of pedagogy. Dr. Silberstein, who served as JLI's Dean of

Curriculum with remarkable dedication and expertise, has moved on to pursue personal objectives. We join our staff and affiliates worldwide in expressing our heartfelt appreciation for Dr. Silberstein's exceptional directorship and dedication and wish her much success in the future.

Rabbi Dr. Daniel Schonbuch served as professional consultant for this course. His ideas and suggestions, based on his years of practical expertise in the field of couple's therapy, enhanced the product. We'd also like to thank **Mrs. Shimona Tzukernik** and **Mrs. Michla Schanowitz** for reviewing the document and providing meaningful comments and critique.

Many thanks to the copyediting team: **Mrs. Chava Shapiro**, **Mrs. Rachel Witty**, and **Mrs. Miriam Levy-Haim Nikaiyn**, who also served, with much dedication, as managing editor of the project.

JLI's talented production team is responsible for the outstanding quality of our printed materials: **Rabbi Mendel Sirota**, production manager; **Nachman Levine**, layout designer; **Spotlight Design**; and **Shimon Leib Jacobs**, who oversees our printing.

Neria Cohen heads our new flagship multimedia team, designing an exemplary integrated project with the collaboration of **Mrs. Chava Shapiro** and **Ms. Nechama Rivka Dubov**. Thanks also to **Moshe Raskin** and **Rabbi Levi Teldon** for video production and **Rabbi Avrohom Bergstein** for assistance with PowerPoint design.

Critical to our success and growth is the hardworking support staff at JLI Central: **Rabbi Zalman Abraham**, Director of Marketing; **Rabbi Mendel Bell,** who ensures the integrity of our online environment; and, lastly, **Rabbi Dubi Rabinowitz**, our chief operating officer.

We are immensely grateful for the encouragement of our chairman and vice-chairman of Merkos L'inyonei Chinuch—Lubavitch World Headquarters, **Rabbi Moshe Kotlarsky**. We are blessed to have the unwavering support of JLI's principal benefactor, **Mr. George Rohr**, who has fully invested in our work and has been instrumental in achieving the monumental expansion of the organization.

JLI's dedicated executive board—**Rabbis Chaim Block, Hesh Epstein, Yosef Gansburg, Shmuel Kaplan, Yisrael Rice,** and **Avrohom Sternberg**—devote countless hours to the development of JLI. Their dedicated commitment and sage direction have helped JLI continue to grow and flourish.

Finally, JLI represents an incredible partnership of more than 300 *shluchim* giving of their time and talent to further Jewish adult education. We thank them for generously sharing their feedback. They are our most valuable critics and our most cherished contributors.

Inspired by the call of the **Lubavitcher Rebbe**, of righteous memory, it is the mandate of the Rohr JLI to encourage all Jews throughout the world to experience and take part in the Torah learning that is their heritage. May this course succeed in fulfilling that sacred charge.

On behalf of the Rohr Jewish Learning Institute,

Efraim Mintz, Executive Director
Yisrael Rice, Chairman, Editorial Board
11 Nisan, 5772

The **Rohr Jewish Learning Institute**

An affiliate of
Merkos L'Inyonei Chinuch
The Educational Arm of
The Chabad Lubavitch Movement
822 Eastern Parkway, Brooklyn, NY 11213

Rabbi Hesh Epstein
Columbia, SC

Rabbi Zalman Aaron Kantor
Mission Viejo, CA

Rabbi Levi Kaplan
Brooklyn, NY

Rabbi Yakov Latowicz
Ventura, CA

Rabbi Yosef Loschak
Goleta, CA

Rabbi Levi Mendelow
Stamford, CT

Rabbi Benzion Milecki
Dover Heights, AU

Rabbi Yossi Nemes
Metairie, LA

Rabbi Reuven New
Boca Raton, FL

Rabbi Dr. Shlomo Pereira
Richmond, VA

Rabbi Shalom Raichik
Gaithersburg, MD

Rabbi Benny Rapoport
Clarks Summit, PA

Rabbi Nochum Schapiro
Sydney, AU

Rabbi Shraga Sherman
Merion Station, PA

Rabbi Avraham Steinmetz
S. Paulo, BR

Rabbi Avrohom Sternberg
New London, CT

Rabbi Aryeh Weinstein
Newtown, PA

Rabbi Motti Wilhelm
Portland, OR

Multimedia Development
Ms. Neria Cohen
Director

Rabbi Avrohom Bergstein
Ms. Nechoma Rivkah Dubov
Rabbi Chesky Edelman
Moshe Raskin
Mrs. Chava Shapiro
Mrs. Leah-Perl Shollar
Rabbi Levi Teldon

Administration
Mrs. Chana Dechter
Mrs. Mindy Wallach

Affiliate Support
Rabbi Mendel Sirota
Mrs. Musie Kesselman
Mrs. Fraydee Kessler
Mrs. Mindy Wallach

Online Division
Rabbi Mendel Bell
Rabbi Hershy Korik
Rabbi Mendel Sirota

Marketing and Branding
Rabbi Zalman Abraham
Director

Marketing Committee
Rabbi Simcha Backman
Glendale, CA

Rabbi Ronnie Fine
Montreal, QC

Rabbi Ovadia Goldman
Oklahoma City, OK

Rabbi Mendy Halberstam
Miami Beach, FL
Rabbi Reuven New
Boca Raton, FL

Rabbi Yehuda Shemtov
Yardley, PA

Marketing Consultants
Scott Dubin
Dubin Strategy and Consulting LLC
Toronto, ON

JJ Gross
New York, NY

Warren Modlin
MednetPro, Inc.
Alpharetta, GA

Alan Rosenspan
Alan Rosenspan & Associates
Sharon, MA

Gary Wexler
Passion Marketing
Los Angeles, CA

Shaul Weisband
Israel

Graphic Design
Spotlight Design
Brooklyn, NY

Friedman Advertising
Los Angeles, CA

Yossi Graphic Design
Brooklyn, NY

Publication Design
Nachman Levine
Detroit, MI
Chazak Publishing House
Kiryat Malachi, Israel

Printing
Shimon Leib Jacobs
Point One Communications
Montreal, QC
Chazak Publishing House
Kiryat Malachi, Israel

Shipping
Mary Stevens
Nixa, MO

Accounting
Ms. Musie Karp
Mrs. Shaina B. Mintz
Mrs. Nechama Shmotkin

JLI Departments
Rabbi Dubi Rabinowitz
Chief Operating Officer

JLI Flagship
Rabbi Yisrael Rice
Chairman
S. Rafael, CA

Rabbi Mordechai Dinerman
Rabbi Naftali Silberberg
Editors

Mrs. Leah-Perl Shollar
Instructional Designer

Rabbi Mendel Sirota
Production Manager

Mrs. Miriam Levy-Haim Nikaiyn
Managing Editor

Mrs. Chava Shapiro
Copy Editor

Mrs. Rachel Witty
Proofreader

Department of Continuing Education
Mrs. Mindy Wallach
Director

Ms. Musie Karp
Registrar

Mrs. Rivka Sternberg
Administrative Support

Dr. Michael Akerman, MD
Consultant
Continuing Medical Education
Associate Professor of Medicine,
SUNY–Downstate Medical Center

JLI for Teens
in partnership with
CTeeN: Chabad Teen Network

Rabbi Chaim Block
Chairman
San Antonio, TX

Rabbi Benny Rapoport
Director
Clarks Summit, PA

Mrs. Gani Goodman
Administrator

Rabbi Beryl Frankel
Director, CTeeN
Yardley, PA

JLI International Desk

Rabbi Avrohom Sternberg
Chairman
New London, CT

Rabbi Yossi Baitsh
Administrator, JLI Israel
In Partnership with
Tzeirei Agudas Chabad

Rabbi Eli Wolf
Administrator, JLI in the CIS
In Parternship with the Federation of
Jewish Communities of the CIS

Rabbi Yitzchak Marton
Regional Representative
Israel

Rabbi Avraham Golovacheov
German Division

Rabbi Nochum Schapiro
Regional Respresentative
Australia

Rabbi Hirshel Hendel
Regional Representative
Spanish Division

myShiur:
Advanced Learning Initiative

Rabbi Shmuel Kaplan
Chairman
Potomac, MD

Rabbi Levi Kaplan
Director

Rosh Chodesh Society

Rabbi Shmuel Kaplan
Chairman
Potomac, MD

Mrs. Shaindy Jacobson
Director

Mrs. Musie Kesselman
Administrator

Steering Committee
Mrs. Rochel Holzkenner
Mrs. Devorah Kornfeld
Mrs. Chana Lipskar
Mrs. Ahuva New
Mrs. Binie Tenenbaum

National Jewish Retreat

Rabbi Hesh Epstein
Chairman
Columbia, SC

Rabbi Boruch Cohen
Director

Bruce Backman
Coordinator

Mrs. Shaina B. Mintz
Administrator

Rabbi Mendy Weg
Founding Director

Sinai Scholars Society
in partnership with
Chabad on Campus

Rabbi Menachem Schmidt
Chairman
Philadelphia, PA

Rabbi Yitzchok Dubov
Director

Devorah Balarsky
Administrator

Executive Committee
Rabbi Moshe Chaim Dubrowski
Rabbi Efraim Mintz
Rabbi Menachem Schmidt
Dr. Chana Silberstein
Rabbi Nechemia Vogel
Rabbi Eitan Webb

TorahCafe.com
Online Learning

Rabbi Levi Kaplan
Director

Mrs. Miri Birk
Adminisrator

Mrs. Chaya Rosenfeld
Project Manager

Rabbi Simcha Backman
Golan Ben-Oni
Rabbi Leibel Karp
Consultants
Rabbi Mendy Elishevitz
Rabbi Mendel Bell
Onstream Media
Website Development

Rabbi Getzel Raskin
Director of Filming and Editing

Rabbi Elya Silfin
Series Manager
Avrohom Shimon Ezagui
Yosef Kramer
Yehuda Shaffer
Rafi Roston
Nachman Blizinsky
Mendel Serobranski
Filming Crew

Moshe Raskin
Mendel Katzman
Yosef Schmalberg
Video Editing

Torah Studies

Rabbi Yossi Gansburg
Chairman
Toronto, ON

Rabbi Meir Hecht
Director

Rabbi Moshe Teldon
Administrator
Rabbi Levi Fogelman
Rabbi Yaacov Halperin
Rabbi Nechemia Schusterman
Rabbi Ari Sollish
Steering Committee

JLI Academy

Rabbi Hesh Epstein
Chairman

Rabbi Mendel Popack
Director
Rabbi Yoel Caroline
Rabbi Mordechai Grossbaum
Rabbi Levi Mendelow
Steering Committee

Beis Medrosh L'Shluchim
in partnership with
Shluchim Exchange

Rabbi Sholom Zirkind
Administrator

Rabbi Mendy Rabin
Coordinator

Rabbi Mendel Margolin
Producer
Rabbi Simcha Backman
Rabbi Mendy Kotlarsky
Rabbi Efraim Mintz
Steering Committee

JLI Central
Founding Department Heads

Rabbi Zalman Charytan
Acworth, GA

Rabbi Mendel Druk
Cancun, Mexico

Rabbi Menachem Gansburg
Toronto, ON

Rabbi Yoni Katz
Brooklyn, NY

Rabbi Chaim Zalman Levy
New Rochelle, NY

Dr. Chana Silberstein
Ithaca, NY

Rabbi Elchonon Tenenbaum
Napa Valley, CA

Rohr **JLI** Affiliates

Share the **Rohr JLI** experience with friends and relatives worldwide

ALABAMA

BIRMINGHAM
Rabbi Yossi Friedman
205.970.0100

ARIZONA

CHANDLER
Rabbi Mendel Deitsch
480.855.4333

FLAGSTAFF
Rabbi Dovie Shapiro
928.255.5756

GLENDALE
Rabbi Sholom Lew
602.375.2422

PHOENIX
Rabbi Zalman Levertov
Rabbi Yossi Friedman
602.944.2753

SCOTTSDALE
Rabbi Yossi Levertov
Rabbi Yossi Bryski
480.998.1410

ARKANSAS

LITTLE ROCK
Rabbi Pinchus Ciment
501.217.0053

CALIFORNIA

AGOURA HILLS
Rabbi Moshe Bryski
818.991.0991

BEL AIR
Rabbi Chaim Mentz
310.475.5311

BEVERLY HILLS
Rabbi Chaim I. Sperlin
310.734.9079

BRENTWOOD
Rabbi Boruch Hecht
Rabbi Mordechai Zaetz
310.826.4453

BURBANK
Rabbi Shmuly Kornfeld
818.954.0070

CALABASAS
Rabbi Eliyahu Friedman
818.585.1888

CARLSBAD
Rabbi Yeruchem Eilfort
Rabbi Michoel Shapiro
760.943.8891

CHATSWORTH
Rabbi Yossi Spritzer
818.718.0777

CONTRA COSTA
Rabbi Yaakov Kagan
Rabbi Dovber Berkowitz
925.937.4101

ENCINO
Rabbi Joshua Gordon
Rabbi Eli Rivkin
818.758.1818

FOLSOM
Rabbi Yossi Grossbaum
916.608.9811

GLENDALE
Rabbi Simcha Backman
818.240.2750

HUNTINGTON BEACH
Rabbi Aron Berkowitz
714.846.2285

IRVINE
Rabbi Alter Tenenbaum
Rabbi Elly Andrusier
949.786.5000

LA JOLLA
Rabbi Baruch Shalom Ezagui
858.455.5433

LAGUNA BEACH
Rabbi Elimelech Gurevitch
949.499.0770

LOMITA
Rabbi Eli Hecht
Rabbi Sholom Pinson
310.326.8234

LONG BEACH
Rabbi Abba Perelmuter
562.621.9828

LOS ANGELES
Rabbi Leibel Korf
323.660.5177

MARINA DEL REY
Rabbi Danny Yiftach
Rabbi Mendy Avtzon
310.859.0770

NEWPORT BEACH
Rabbi Reuven Mintz
949.721.9800

NORTH HOLLYWOOD
Rabbi Nachman Abend
818.989.9539

NORTHRIDGE
Rabbi Eli Rivkin
818.368.3937

PACIFIC PALISADES
Rabbi Zushe Cunin
310.454.7783

PALO ALTO
Rabbi Menachem Landa
CLASSES IN HEBREW
650.322.1708

PASADENA
Rabbi Chaim Hanoka
626.564.8820

RANCHO CUCAMONGA
Rabbi Sholom B. Harlig
909.949.4553

RANCHO PALOS VERDES
Rabbi Yitzchok Magalnic
310.544.5544

RANCHO S. FE
Rabbi Levi Raskin
858.756.7571

REDONDO BEACH
Rabbi Dovid Lisbon
310.214.4999

REDWOOD CITY
Rabbi Levi Potash
650.232.0995

SACRAMENTO
Rabbi Mendy Cohen
916.455.1400

S. BARBARA
Rabbi Yosef Loschak
805.683.1544

S. CLEMENTE
Rabbi Menachem M. Slavin
949.489.0723

S. CRUZ
Rabbi Yochanan Friedman
831.454.0101

S. DIEGO
Rabbi Motte Fradkin
858.547.0076

S. DIEGO-UNIVERSITY CITY
Rabbi Yudell Reiz
619.723.2439

S. FRANCISCO
Rabbi Peretz Mochkin
415.571.8770

S. MONICA
Rabbi Boruch Rabinowitz
310.394.5699

S. RAFAEL
Rabbi Yisrael Rice
415.492.1666

SIMI VALLEY
Rabbi Nosson Gurary
805.577.0573

STOCKTON
Rabbi Avremel Brod
209.952.2081

STUDIO CITY
Rabbi Yossi Baitelman
818.508.6633

TEMECULA
Rabbi Yitzchok Hurwitz
951.303.9576

THOUSAND OAKS
Rabbi Chaim Bryski
805.493.7776

TUSTIN
Rabbi Yehoshua Eliezrie
714.508.2150

VENTURA
Rabbi Yakov Latowicz
Mrs. Sarah Latowicz
805.658.7441

WEST HILLS
Rabbi Avrahom Yitzchak Rabin
818.337.4544

YORBA LINDA
Rabbi Dovid Eliezrie
714.693.0770

COLORADO
ASPEN
Rabbi Mendel Mintz
970.544.3770

BOULDER
Rabbi Pesach Scheiner
303.494.1638

DENVER
Rabbi Yossi Serebryanski
303.744.9699

HIGHLANDS RANCH
Rabbi Avraham Mintz
303.694.9119

LONGMONT
Rabbi Yaakov Dovid Borenstein
303.678.7595

VAIL
Rabbi Dovid Mintz
970.476.7887

WESTMINSTER
Rabbi Benjy Brackman
303.429.5177

CONNECTICUT
GLASTONBURY
Rabbi Yosef Wolvovsky
860.659.2422

GREENWICH
Rabbi Yossi Deren
Rabbi Menachem Feldman
203.629.9059

NEW LONDON
Rabbi Avrohom Sternberg
860.437.8000

ORANGE
Rabbi Sheya Hecht
Rabbi Adam Haston
203.795.5261

SIMSBURY
Rabbi Mendel Samuels
860.658.4903

STAMFORD
Rabbi Yisrael Deren
Rabbi Levi Mendelow
203.3.CHABAD

WEST HARTFORD
Rabbi Yosef Gopin
Rabbi Shaya Gopin
860.659.2422

WESTPORT
Rabbi Yehuda L. Kantor
Mrs. Dina Kantor
203.226.8584

DELAWARE
WILMINGTON
Rabbi Chuni Vogel
302.529.9900

FLORIDA
AVENTURA
Rabbi Laivi Forta
Rabbi Yakov Garfinkel
305.933.0770

BAL HARBOUR
Rabbi Dov Schochet
305.868.1411

BOCA RATON
Rabbi Moishe Denberg
Rabbi Zalman Bukiet
561.417.7797

BOYNTON BEACH
Rabbi Yosef Yitzchok Raichik
561.732.4633

BRADENTON
Rabbi Menachem Bukiet
941.388.9656

CORAL GABLES
Rabbi Avrohom Stolik
305.490.7572

DEERFIELD BEACH
Rabbi Yossi Goldblatt
954.422.1735

DELRAY BEACH
Rabbi Sholom Ber Korf
561.496.6228

EAST BOCA RATON
Rabbi Ruvi New
561.417.7797

FORT LAUDERDALE
Rabbi Yitzchok Naparstek
954.568.1190

FORT MYERS
Rabbi Yitzchok Minkowicz
Mrs. Nechama Minkowicz
239.433.7708

HOLLYWOOD
Rabbi Leizer Barash
954.965.9933

KENDALL
Rabbi Yossi Harlig
305.234.5654

KEY BISCAYNE
Rabbi Yoel Caroline
305.365.6744

KEY WEST
Rabbi Yaakov Zucker
305.295.0013

MIAMI–MIDTOWN
Rabbi Shmuel Gopin
305.573.9995

NAPLES
Rabbi Fishel Zaklos
239.262.4474

NORTH MIAMI BEACH
Rabbi Moishe Kievman
305.770.1919

ORLANDO
Rabbi Yosef Konikov
407.354.3660

PARKLAND
Rabbi Mendy Gutnik
954.796.7330

PINELLAS COUNTY
Rabbi Shalom Adler
727.789.0408

PLANTATION
Rabbi Pinchas Taylor
954.644.9177

SARASOTA
Rabbi Chaim Shaul Steinmetz
941.925.0770

SATELLITE BEACH
Rabbi Zvi Konikov
321.777.2770

SOUTH PALM BEACH
Rabbi Leibel Stolik
561.889.3499

SOUTH TAMPA
Rabbi Mendy Dubrowski
813.287.1795

SUNNY ISLES BEACH
Rabbi Alexander Kaller
305.803.5315

TALLAHASSEE
Rabbi Schneur Zalmen Oirechman
850.523.9294

VENICE
Rabbi Sholom Ber Schmerling
941.493.2770

WALNUT CREEK
Rabbi Zalman Korf
954.374.8370

WESTON
Rabbi Yisroel Spalter
954.349.6565

WEST PALM BEACH
Rabbi Yoel Gancz
561.659.7770

WEST PASCO
Rabbi Yossi Eber
727.376.3366

GEORGIA
ALPHARETTA
Rabbi Hirshy Minkowicz
770.410.9000

ATLANTA
Rabbi Yossi New
Rabbi Isser New
404.843.2464

ATLANTA: INTOWN
Rabbi Eliyahu Schusterman
Rabbi Ari Sollish
404.898.0434

GWINNETT
Rabbi Yossi Lerman
678.595.0196

Marietta
Rabbi Ephraim Silverman
Rabbi Zalman Charytan
770.565.4412

IDAHO
Boise
Rabbi Mendel Lifshitz
208.853.9200

ILLINOIS
Champaign
Rabbi Dovid Tiechtel
217.355.8672

Chicago
Rabbi Meir Hecht
312.714.4655

Chicago-Hyde Park
Rabbi Yossi Brackman
773.955.8672

Gurnee
Rabbi Sholom Ber Tenenbaum
847.782.1800

Glenview
Rabbi Yishaya Benjaminson
847.998.9896

Highland Park
Mrs. Michla Schanowitz
847.266.0770

Naperville
Rabbi Mendy Goldstein
630.778.9770

Northbrook
Rabbi Meir Moscowitz
847.564.8770
Rabbi Menachem Slavaticki
Classes in Hebrew
847.350.9770

Oak Park
Rabbi Yitzchok Bergstein
708.524.1530

Peoria
Rabbi Eli Langsam
309.692.2250

Skokie
Rabbi Yochanan Posner
847.677.1770

Wilmette
Rabbi Dovid Flinkenstein
847.251.7707

INDIANA
Indianapolis
Rabbi Mendel Schusterman
317.251.5573

KANSAS
Overland Park
Rabbi Mendy Wineberg
913.649.4852

LOUISIANA
Metairie
Rabbi Yossi Nemes
504.454.2910

MARYLAND
Baltimore
Rabbi Elchonon Lisbon
410.358.4787

Rabbi Velvel Belinsky
Classes in Russian
410.764.5000

Bethesda
Rabbi Bentzion Geisinsky
Rabbi Sender Geisinsky
301.913.9777

Columbia
Rabbi Hillel Baron
Rabbi Yosef Chaim Sufrin
410.740.2424

Gaithersburg
Rabbi Sholom Raichik
301.926.3632

Potomac
Rabbi Mendel Bluming
301.983.4200

Silver Spring
Rabbi Berel Wolvovsky
301.593.1117

MASSACHUSETTS
Amherst
Rabbi Shmuel Kravitsky
413.835.0085

Hyannis
Rabbi Yekusiel Alperowitz
508.775.2324

Longmeadow
Rabbi Yakov Wolff
413.567.8665

Sudbury
Rabbi Yisroel Freeman
978.443.3691

Swampscott
Mrs. Layah Lipsker
781.581.3833

Westborough
Rabbi Michoel Green
508.366.0499

MICHIGAN
Ann Arbor
Rabbi Aharon Goldstein
734.995.3276

Grand Rapids
Rabbi Mordechai Haller
616.957.0770

Novi
Rabbi Avrohom Susskind
248.790.6075

West Bloomfield
Rabbi Kasriel Shemtov
248.788.4000

Rabbi Elimelech Silberberg
Rabbi Avrohom Wineberg
248.855 .6170

MINNESOTA
Minnetonka
Rabbi Mordechai Grossbaum
952.929.9922

Rochester
Rabbi Dovid Greene
507.288.7500

S. Paul
Rabbi Shneur Zalman Bendet
651.278.8401

MISSOURI
S. Louis
Rabbi Yosef Landa
314.725.0400

MONTANA
Bozeman
Rabbi Chaim Shaul Bruk
406.585.8770

NEBRASKA
Omaha
Rabbi Mendel Katzman
402.330.1800

NEVADA
Henderson
Rabbi Mendy Harlig
Rabbi Tzvi Bronstein
702.617.0770

Summerlin
Rabbi Yisroel Schanowitz
Rabbi Tzvi Bronstein
702.855.0770

NEW JERSEY
Basking Ridge
Rabbi Mendy Herson
908.604.8844

Cherry Hill
Rabbi Mendy Mangel
856.874.1500

Clinton
Rabbi Eli Kornfeld
908.623.7000

Fort Lee
Rabbi Meir Konikov
201.886.1238

Franklin Lakes
Rabbi Chanoch Kaplan
201.848.0449

Hillsborough
Rabbi Shmaya Krinsky
908.874.0444

Holmdel
Rabbi Shmaya Galperin
732.772.1998

Madison
Rabbi Shalom Lubin
973.377.0707

MANALAPAN
Rabbi Boruch Chazanow
732.972.3687

MEDFORD
Rabbi Yitzchok Kahan
609.953.3150

MOUNTAIN LAKES
Rabbi Levi Dubinsky
973.551.1898

NORTH BRUNSWICK
Rabbi Levi Azimov
732.398.9492

OLD TAPPAN
Rabbi Mendy Lewis
201.767.4008

RANDOLPH
Rabbi Avraham Bechor
973.895.3070

ROCKAWAY
Rabbi Asher Herson
Rabbi Mordechai Baumgarten
973.625.1525

SPARTA
Rabbi Shmuel Lewis
973.726.3333

TEANECK
Rabbi Ephraim Simon
201.907.0686

TENAFLY
Rabbi Mordechai Shain
Rabbi Yitzchak Gershovitz
201.871.1152

TOMS RIVER
Rabbi Moshe Gourarie
732.349.4199

WEST ORANGE
Rabbi Mendy Kasowitz
973.731.0770

WOODCLIFF LAKE
Rabbi Dov Drizin
201.476.0157

NEW MEXICO
S. FE
Rabbi Berel Levertov
505.983.2000

NEW YORK
ALBANY
Rabbi Yossi Rubin
518.482.5781

BEDFORD
Rabbi Arik Wolf
914.666.6065

BINGHAMTON
Mrs. Rivkah Slonim
607.797.0015

BRIGHTON BEACH
Rabbi Zushe Winner
Rabbi Avrohom Winner
718.946.9833

BROOKLYN
Mrs. Shimona Tzukernik
718.493.2859

DIX HILLS
Rabbi Yaakov Saacks
631.351.8672

DOBBS FERRY
Rabbi Benjy Silverman
914.693.6100

EAST HAMPTON
Rabbi Leibel Baumgarten
631.329.5800

GREAT NECK
Rabbi Yoseph Geisinsky
516.487.4554

ITHACA
Rabbi Eli Silberstein
607.257.7379

KINGSTON
Rabbi Yitzchok Hecht
845.334.9044

LARCHMONT
Rabbi Mendel Silberstein
914.834.4321

LONG BEACH
Rabbi Eli Goodman
Rabbi Mendel Popack
516.897.2473

NYC TRIBECA
Rabbi S. Zalman Paris
646.510.3109

NYC WEST SIDE
Rabbi Yisrael Kugel
212.799.0809

NYC GRAMERCY PARK
Rabbi Naftali Rotenstreich
212.924.3200

NYC KEHILATH JESHURUN
Rabbi Elie Weinstock
212.774.5636

OSSINING
Rabbi Dovid Labkowski
914.923.2522

PORT WASHINGTON
Rabbi Shalom Paltiel
516.767.8672

RIVERDALE
Rabbi Levi Shemtov
718.549.1100

ROCHESTER
Rabbi Nechemia Vogel
585.271.0330

ROSLYN
Rabbi Yaakov Reiter
516.484.8185

SEA GATE
Rabbi Chaim Brikman
Mrs. Rivka Brikman
718.266.1736

STATEN ISLAND
Rabbi Moshe Katzman
Rabbi Shmuel Bendet
718.370.8953

Rabbi Nachman Segal
CLASSES IN HEBREW
718. 761.4483

STONY BROOK
Rabbi Shalom Ber Cohen
631.585.0521

WEST HEMPSTEAD
Rabbi Yossi Lieberman
Rabbi Mordechai Dinerman
516.596.8691

WOODBURY
Rabbi Shmuel Lipszyc
516.682.0404

NORTH CAROLINA
ASHEVILLE
Rabbi Shaya Susskind
828.505.0746

CHAPEL HILL
Rabbi Zalman Bluming
919.630.5129

CHARLOTTE
Rabbi Yossi Groner
Rabbi Shlomo Cohen
704.366.3984

GREENSBORO
Rabbi Yosef Plotkin
336 617 8120

RALEIGH
Rabbi Aaron Herman
919.637.6950

Rabbi Pinchas Herman
Rabbi Sholom Ber Estrin
919.847.8986

OHIO
BEACHWOOD
Rabbi Yossi Marosov
216.381.4736

BLUE ASH
Rabbi Yisroel Mangel
513.793.5200

COLUMBUS
Rabbi Areyah Kaltmann
Rabbi Levi Andrusier
614.294.3296

DAYTON
Rabbi Nochum Mangel
Rabbi Dr. Shmuel Klatzkin
937.643.0770

TOLEDO
Rabbi Yossi Shemtov
419.843.9393

OKLAHOMA
OKLAHOMA CITY
Rabbi Ovadia Goldman
405.524.4800

TULSA
Rabbi Yehuda Weg
918.492.4499

OREGON
ASHLAND
Rabbi Avi Zwiebel
541.482.2778

PORTLAND
Rabbi Moshe Wilhelm
Rabbi Mordechai Wilhelm
503.977.9947

PENNSYLVANIA
AMBLER
Rabbi Shaya Deitsch
215.591.9310

BALA CYNWYD
Rabbi Shraga Sherman
610.660.9192

FOX CHAPEL
Rabbi Ely Rosenfeld
412.781.1800

CLARKS SUMMIT
Rabbi Benny Rapoport
570.587.3300

DEVON
Rabbi Yossi Kaplan
610.971.9977

LANCASTER
Rabbi Elazar Green
717.368.6565

NEWTOWN
Rabbi Aryeh Weinstein
215.497.9925

PHILADELPHIA: CENTER CITY
Rabbi Yochonon Goldman
215.238.2100

PITTSBURGH
Rabbi Yisroel Altein
412.422.7300 ext. 269

PITTSBURGH: SOUTH HILLS
Rabbi Mendy Rosenblum
412.278.3693

READING
Rabbi Yosef Lipsker
610.921.2805

RYDAL
Rabbi Zushe Gurevitz
215.572.1511

WYNNEWOOD
Rabbi Moishe Brennan
610.529.9011

RHODE ISLAND
WARWICK
Rabbi Yossi Laufer
401.884.7888

SOUTH CAROLINA
COLUMBIA
Rabbi Hesh Epstein
803.782.1831

TENNESSEE
CHATTANOOGA
Rabbi Shaul Perlstein
423.490.1106

KNOXVILLE
Rabbi Yossi Wilhelm
865.588.8584

MEMPHIS
Rabbi Levi Klein
901.766.1800

NASHVILLE
Rabbi Yitzchok Tiechtel
615.646.5750

TEXAS
ARLINGTON
Rabbi Levi Gurevitch
817.451.1171

DALLAS
Rabbi Peretz Shapiro
Rabbi Moshe Naparstek
972.818.0770

FORT WORTH
Rabbi Dov Mandel
817.263.7701

HOUSTON
Rabbi Moishe Traxler
713.774.0300

HOUSTON: RICE UNIVERSITY AREA
Rabbi Eliezer Lazaroff
Rabbi Yitzchok Schmukler
713.522.2004

PLANO
Rabbi Mendel Block
Rabbi Yehudah Horowitz
972.596.8270

S. ANTONIO
Rabbi Chaim Block
Rabbi Yossi Marrus
210.492.1085

UTAH
SALT LAKE CITY
Rabbi Benny Zippel
801.467.7777

VERMONT
BURLINGTON
Rabbi Yitzchok Raskin
802.658.5770

VIRGINIA
ALEXANDRIA/ARLINGTON
Rabbi Mordechai Newman
703.370.2774

FAIRFAX
Rabbi Leibel Fajnland
703.426.1980

NORFOLK
Rabbi Aaron Margolin
Rabbi Levi Brashevitzky
757.616.0770

RICHMOND
Rabbi Dr. Shlomo Pereira
804.740.2000

TYSONS CORNER
Chapter founded by
Rabbi Levi Deitsch, OBM

Rabbi Chezzy Deitsch
703.829.5770

WASHINGTON
BELLEVUE
Rabbi Mordechai Farkash
Rabbi Sholom Ber Elishevitz
425.957.7860

OLYMPIA
Rabbi Cheski Edelman
360.584-4306

SEATTLE
Rabbi Elazar Bogomilsky
206.527.1411

SPOKANE COUNTY
Rabbi Yisroel Hahn
509.443.0770

WISCONSIN
MEQUON
Rabbi Menachem Rapoport
262.242.2235

MILWAUKEE
Rabbi Mendel Shmotkin
414.961.6100

PUERTO RICO
CAROLINA
Rabbi Mendel Zarchi
787.253.0894

ARGENTINA
BUENOS AIRES
BELGRANO-OLLEROS
Rabbi Mendy Birman
54.11.4774.5071

PALERMO NUEVO
Rabbi Mendy Grunblatt
54.11.4772.1024

RECOLETA
Rabbi Hirshel Hendel
54.11.4807.7073

VILLA DEL PARQUE
Rabbi Yosef Itzjok Levy
54.11.4504.1908

AUSTRALIA
BONDI
Rabbi Pinchas Feldman
Rabbi Eli Feldman
612.9387.3822

BRISBANE
Rabbi Chanoch Sufrin
617.3843.6770

DOUBLE BAY
Rabbi Yanky Berger
612.9327.1644

DOVER HEIGHTS
Rabbi Benzion Milecki
612.9337.6775

MELBOURNE
Rabbi Schneier Lange
613.9522.8222

Rabbi Shimshon Yurkowicz
613.9822.3600

NORTH SHORE
Rabbi Nochum Schapiro
Mrs. Fruma Schapiro
612.9488.9548

SYDNEY
Rabbi Levi Wolff
612.9389.5622

VICTORIA
SOUTH YARRA
Rabbi Yehuda Hoch
03.9613.0738

BELARUS
GRODNO
Rabbi Yitzchak Kofman
375.29.6443690

BRAZIL
RIO DE JANEIRO
Rabbi Yehoshua Goldman
Rabbi Avraham Steinmetz
55.21.3543.3770

S. PAULO
Rabbi Avraham Steinmetz
55.11.3081.3081

CANADA
ALBERTA
CALGARY
Rabbi Mordechai Groner
403.238.4880

EDMONTON
Rabbi Ari Drelich
Rabbi Mendy Blachman
780.851.1515

BRITISH COLUMBIA
RICHMOND
Rabbi Yechiel Baitelman
604.277.6427

VICTORIA
Rabbi Meir Kaplan
250.595.7656

MANITOBA
WINNIPEG
Rabbi Avrohom Altein
Rabbi Shmuel Altein
204.339.8737

ONTARIO
Lawrence/Eglinton
Rabbi Menachem Gansburg
416.546.8770

LONDON
Rabbi Eliezer Gurkow
519.434.3962

MISSISSAUGA
Rabbi Yitzchok Slavin
905.820.4432

NIAGARA FALLS
Rabbi Zalman Zaltzman

OTTAWA
Rabbi Menachem M. Blum
613.823.0866

Richmond Hill
Rabbi Mendel Bernstein
905.770.7700

Toronto
Rabbi Yisroel Landa
CLASSES IN HEBREW
905.709.7770

TORONTO AREA
BJL
Rabbi Leib Chaiken
416.916.7202

Greater Toronto
REGIONAL OFFICE & THORNHILL
Rabbi Yossi Gansburg
905.731.7000

YORK MILLS
Rabbi Levi Gansburg
647.345.3800

YORK UNIVERSITY
Rabbi Vidal Bekerman
416.856.4575

QUEBEC
MONTREAL
Rabbi Ronnie Fine
Rabbi Leibel Fine
514.342.3.JLI

TOWN OF MOUNT ROYAL
Rabbi Moshe Krasnanski
514.739.0770

VILLE S. LAURENT
Rabbi Schneur Zalmen Silberstein
514.808.1418

COLOMBIA
BOGOTA
Rabbi Yehoshua B. Rosenfeld
Rabbi Chanoch Piekarski
571.635.8251

DENMARK
COPENHAGEN
Rabbi Yitzchok Lowenthal
45.3316.1850

ESTONIA
TALLINN
Rabbi Shmuel Kot
372.662.30.50

GEORGIA
TBILISI
Rabbi Meir Kozlovsky
995.593.23.91.15

GERMANY
BERLIN
Rabbi Yehuda Tiechtel
4930.212.808.30

MUNICH
Rabbi Yochonon Gordon
49.89.4190.2812

COLOGNE
Rabbi Mendel Schtroks
49.221.240.3902

GREECE
ATHENS
Rabbi Mendel Hendel
30.210.520.2880

GUATEMALA
GUATEMALA CITY
Rabbi Shalom Pelman
502.2485.0770

ISRAEL
ARIEL
Rabbi Sasson Carmel
03.6039937

ASHDOD
Rabbi Yosef Friedman
052.4240675

ASHKELON
Rabbi Shneor Lieberman
054.9770512

BALFURYA
Rabbi Noam Bar-Tov
054.5804770

BE'ER YA'AKOV
Rabbi Shmuel Bekerman
08.9282158

CAESAREA
Rabbi Chaim Meir Lieberman
054.6212586

EVEN YEHUDA
Rabbi Menachem Noyman
054.7770707

GANEI TIKVA
Rabbi Gershon Shnur
054.5242358

GIV'ATAYIM
Rabbi Pinchus Bitton
052.6438770

HADERA
Rabbi Baruch Bekerman
054-2577028

HAIFA
Rabbi Yehuda Dunin
054.4263763

HOLON
Rabbi Shmuel Raskin
054.5770000

JERUSALEM
Rabbi Eliyahu Canterman
CLASSES IN ENGLISH
054.6823737

KARMIEL
Rabbi Mendy Elishevitz
054.5213073

KIRYAT BIALIK
Rabbi Pinny Marton
050.6611768

KIRYAT MOTZKIN
Rabbi Shimon Eizenbach
050.9020770

KIRYAT YAM
Rabbi Aharon Gopin
054.2577044

Maccabim Re'ut
Rabbi Yosef Yitzchak Noiman
054.9770549

Nes Ziyona
Rabbi Menachem Feldman
054.4977092

Netanya
Rabbi Schneur Brod
054.5797572

Ramat Yishai
Rabbi Shneor Zalman Wolosow
052.3245475

Rishon Lezion
Rabbi Uri Keshet
050.7224593

Zikhron Ya'akov
Rabbi Yosef Yitzchak Freiman
054.6631770

NETHERLANDS
Den Haag
Rabbi Shmuel Katzman
31.70.347.0222

PANAMA
Panama City
Rabbi Ari Laine
Rabbi Gabriel Benayon
507.223.3383

RUSSIA
Samara
Rabbi Shlomo Deutch
7.846.333.40.64

Saratov
Rabbi Yaakov Kubitshek
Rabbi Asaf Feinstein
7.8452.21.58.00

S. Petersburg
Rabbi Zvi Pinsky
7.812.713.62.09

Rostov
Rabbi Chaim Danziger
7.8632.99.02.68

Ulyanovsk
Rabbi Yossi Marozov

SINGAPORE
Singapore
Rabbi Mordechai Abergel
656.337.2189

SOUTH AFRICA
Cape Town
Rabbi Mendel Popack
Rabbi Pinchas Hecht
27.21.434.3740

Johannesburg
Rabbi Dovid Hazdan
Rabbi Shmuel Simpson
27.11.728.8152

Rabbi Dovid Masinter
Rabbi Ari Kievman
27.11.440.6600

SWEDEN
Stockholm
Rabbi Chaim Greisman
468.679.7067

SWITZERLAND
Lugano
Rabbi Yaakov Tzvi Kantor
091.921.3720

Luzern
Rabbi Chaim Drukman
414.1361.1770

UNITED KINGDOM
Edgeware
Rabbi Leivi Sudak
Rabbi Yaron Jacobs
44.208.905.4141

Leeds
Rabbi Eli Pink
44.113.266.3311

London
Rabbi Gershon Overlander
Rabbi Dovid Katz
44.208.202.1600

UKRAINE
Cherkassy
Rabbi Dov Axelrod
380.472.45.70.80

Odessa
Rabbi Avraham Wolf
Rabbi Yaakov Neiman
38.048.728.0770 ext. 280

Nikolayev
Rabbi Sholom Gotlieb
380.512.35.55.39

VENEZUELA
Caracas
Rabbi Yehoshua Rosenblum
58.212.264.7011

NOTES

NOTES

NOTES

NOTES

JEWISH LEARNING INSTITUTE

THE JEWISH LEARNING MULTIPLEX

Brought to you by the Rohr Jewish Learning Institute

In fulfillment of the mandate of the Lubavitcher Rebbe, of blessed memory,
whose leadership guides every step of our work,
the mission of the Rohr Jewish Learning Institute is to transform
Jewish life and the greater community through the study of Torah,
connecting each Jew to our shared heritage of Jewish learning.

While our flagship program remains the cornerstone of our organization,
JLI is proud to feature additional divisions catering to specific populations,
in order to meet a wide array of educational needs.

THE ROHR JEWISH LEARNING INSTITUTE,
a subsidiary of *Merkos L'Inyonei Chinuch,*
is the adult education arm of the Chabad-Lubavitch Movement.